D1479166

She Left Nothing in Particular

SHE LEFT NOTHING IN PARTICULAR

The Autobiographical Legacy of
Nineteenth-Century Women's Diaries

AMY L. WINK

THE UNIVERSITY OF TENNESSEE PRESS

KNOXVILLE

Copyright © 2001 by The University of Tennessee Press / Knoxville.
All Rights Reserved. Manufactured in the United States of America.
First Edition.

Chapter 2 originally appeared as "Narratives of Resistance" in
a/b: Auto/Biography Studies 13, no. 2 (1998): 199–222. It is
reprinted by permission.

The paper used in this book meets the minimum requirements of
ANSI/NISO Z39.⁴8-1992 (R 1997) (Permanence of Paper). The
binding materials have been chosen for strength and durability.

Library of Congress Cataloging-in-Publication Data

Wink, Amy L.
She left nothing in particular: the autobiographical legacy of
nineteenth-century women's diaries / Amy L. Wink.—1st ed.
p.   cm.
Includes bibliographical references (p.   ) and index.
ISBN 1-57233-145-3 (hardcover : alk. paper)
1. American diaries—Women authors—History and criticism.
2. American prose literature—19th century—History and
criticism. 3. Women—United States—History—19th
century—Historiography. 4. Women and literature—United
States—History—19th century. 5. Women—United States—
Biography—History and criticism. 6. Autobiography—
Women authors.
I. Title.
PS409 .W56 2001
818'.303099287—dc21   2001000820

TO MY PARENTS, ED AND WINIFRED WINK,

AND MAGGIE

Bless the gift of memory
that breaks unbidden, released
from a flower or a cup of tea
so the dead move like rain through the room.

MARGE PIERCY, "AMIDAH: ON
OUR FEET WE SPEAK TO YOU"

CONTENTS

ACKNOWLEDGMENTS

I would like to thank Suzanne Bunkers, Pamela Matthews, Russell Meyer, Mary D. Robertson, Janis Stout, and Emily Toth for their scholarly advice, professional enthusiasm, and personal support for this project. My thanks go to the librarians and staff of the Center for American History of the University of Texas at Austin for their assistance with these primary materials, as well as my students in my women's autobiography course, and my women's frontier diaries class, whose spirited and powerful questions made the reasons for my work very clear. I would also like to thank Margaret J. M. Ezell, whose steadfast mentoring, unflinching encouragement, and determined belief in my abilities and my work *always* boosted my waning spirits.

She Left Nothing in Particular could not have been completed without the personal support of my family and friends. My gratitude goes to my parents, Ed and Winifred Wink, for their unwavering support. Dad, thanks for your gentle spirit and intellectual curiosity. Mom, thanks for your fiery determination, creativity, and the stamina to make it through this process. Thanks to Marc, Dulcie, and Connor Wink, who have graciously enriched my life with both tangible and intangible gifts and have known how much this work means to me and how difficult it has been. I thank my dear friends who have continued to encourage and humor me through-out the most Sisyphean moments of my career: Julie Campbell; Beth Donaldson; Joel Laurin; Emily, Alex, and Helen Reese; and particularly Sheryl and Michael Mylan, Stacey Short, and Kristi Wright. Sheryl and Mikey, you saved me during the most difficult days; without you, this manuscript would have never been submitted. Stacey, your bold courage, honest rage, sharp and witty tongue, and unfailing belief in my work and my writing has constantly bolstered my energies and spurred me through the darkest times.

Kristi, for many years of our friendship, you have always been a believer. You had faith when I had none and sustained me through those darker moments with your reassurance. Your marvelous wit and humor have always helped me remember to take myself a little less seriously; you always know how and when I need to laugh. For every phone call, card, letter, e-mail, and thought, I can't thank you enough. For knowing how I think and listening to what I think, I am ever grateful and appreciative. For all the small and lovely things which can never be counted and never be written, but which are never forgotten, I thank you. Without you, I do not know how I could have done this work.

Introduction
Reading Women in the Act of Writing

Thought-Woman, the spider,
named things and
as she named them
they appeared.
She is sitting in her room
thinking of a story now

I'm telling you the story
she is thinking.

LESLIE MARMON SILKO, *CEREMONY*

Virginia Woolf's semi-autobiographical story "The Legacy" (published posthumously in 1944) is a paradigmatic story about reading and interpreting diaries. The self-absorbed Gilbert Clandon reads his dead wife Angela's diary as a record of her life with him, "filling in scene after scene of her scrappy details," and thinks it "full of little trifles, the insignificant happy daily trifles that made up her life" (130–31). Through Gilbert's fragmented and disinterested reading, Angela's writing does reveal the turmoil of her life as the wife of a prominent politician: "Did I realize my responsibility, Lady L. asked me, as Gilbert's wife?" She also writes about her own work: "saw Mrs. Jones. . . . She has ten children. . . . Husband lost his arm in an accident. . . . Did my best to find a job for Lily" (132). Her own intellectual interests coalesce as she writes, connecting the material luxury of her life to the poverty she sees during her volunteer work in Whitechapel: "when I think of it I can barely stand to go on living in such luxury. . . . Three guineas for one hat!" (133). Gilbert considers her questions with cursory interest and describes his inheritance, his wife's fifteen-volume diary, as "nothing in particular" (126).

In contrast to Gilbert's trivializing, feminist scholars have viewed women's diaries quite differently, recognizing their significance as forms of women's autobiography and records of women's experiential history. While Estelle Jelinek does not discuss the diary in her early study, *The Tradition of Women's Autobiography* (1986), she notes the accessibility of this autobiographical form for many women, "whose emotional, intellectual, and practical lives are fragmented by domestic responsibilities that leave them little leisure time to contemplate or integrate their experiences" (104). Jelinek's assertion that the diary is *a* form of autobiography available to most women has fueled additional discussions of diaries as a *feminine* form of autobiography.

In her article "Expanding the Boundaries of Criticism: The Diary as Female Autobiography" (1987), Judy Lensink suggests that the diary remains a marginal form of autobiography because the narrative is "both female and ordinary" (40). Cogently arguing for the inclusion of the diary as the text that is "closest to a female version of autobiography" (40), Lensink posits that women create cohesive autobiographies within their diaries by employing literary techniques such as metaphor, character, imagery, and persona. Additionally, Lensink sees particular value in the "nearer truth" of diary texts. She describes reading a woman's journal as similar to "watching a young child at play. If you can catch her in a private moment, you can come close to hearing her real voice. . . . It still poses as a child's, but the private voice is much better" (44). Valorizing the private voices of ordinary women is a collateral intention of feminist interpretations of the diary's autobiographical significance. Penelope Franklin suggests that the diary is a place for a woman "to get in touch with and develop hidden parts of herself — often those aspects for which little support is given by others — and establish emotional stability and independence" (xix). Suzanne Bunkers argues that the diary can be read as "the most authentic form of autobiography because it is least subject to outside editing and censorship and because it most fully represents life as a process" ("Midwestern Diaries," 191).

These arguments accentuate the private act of writing through which the self is revealed to the writer as well as her readers. Estelle Jelinek sees the diary as a fragmented text that reflects a woman's "multidimensional, fragmented self-image" (*Tradition of Women's Autobiography,* xiii). Though the diary does offer an intimate view of a woman's multiplicity, I suggest she may appear "fragmented" only to readers of a text that appears to be "fragmented." As Lensink argues, the diary is not necessarily a fragmented text unless it is viewed with the traditional image of a literary text as a cohesive narrative. However, Lensink also privileges the private voice as "better" than the public voice (44). Describing a woman's "real" voice as childlike, moreover, continues a disturbing patriarchal tendency to infantilize women. Arguing that this private and childlike persona is the "better" representation of a woman is even more problematic. A woman's private self is one aspect of her multiplicity, and to claim her private voice as the "better" representation limits the significance of her public voice and can be construed as an essentialist argument. Additionally, even though diaries are generally private writing, distinguishing between a woman's private and public personas cannot reliably be accomplished. Comprehending the differences between a woman's private and public voices is unfeasible when she is only represented through her private writing; for many ordinary women, the only record of their lives and voices are their diaries. Ascertaining the significant influence a woman's private voice may have had on her public persona is equally difficult. If a woman uses the diary to "get in touch with and develop hidden parts of herself" (Franklin xix), it is logical to assume that these developed aspects of her private self influence her public self.

Despite these difficulties, these interpretations of women's diaries are profitable and intriguing. These readings emphasize the "self" and "life" dimensions of the autobiographical significance of women's diaries, examining specifically how these texts configure a new and expanded definition of auto-biography through the representation of a relatively private female voice. Penelope Franklin and other critics have noted the use of writing as crucial to self-construction. According to Margo Culley, "the diary is an act of language that, by speaking one's self, sustains one's sense of being a self, with autonomous and significant identity" (*A Day at a Time* 5). In this way, the act of writing is a form of resistance to influences which inhibit women's autonomy. As bell hooks explains, "the art of expressing one's feeling on the written page" is connected "with the construction of self and iden-tity" and "the effort to be fully self-actualized" (72). Thus, through writing, women have been able to express and under-stand themselves within a patriarchal system which inhibits and discourages their self-actualization.

In the act of writing is the very "act of saying I" (Didion 17), and these writings are acts to make women's lives mean-ingful to themselves. As Harriet Blodgett suggests, "diary keeping has been practiced so extensively by women because it has been possible for them and gratifying to them" (5). Simply stated, women have kept journals because they liked to. Historian Gayle Davis argues that diaries, specifically those kept by American pioneer women, offer an important insight into women's use of writing as "a significant cop-ing mechanism" (5). Maintaining that their diaries aided women's adjustment to the challenges of frontier travel and existence, Davis suggests that the more a woman's sense of her own identity was threatened by the crude conditions of the frontier, the more reassuring the writing act became in "maintaining" her self-image as a Victorian lady (8). Thus the act of keeping a diary allowed a writer to maintain her "mental equilibrium" through "the order and control" of her writing and to make her experience "tangible, finite, and controllable" (12).

In her article "Toward a Feminist Strategy for Studying Women's Lives," psychological theorist Abigail J. Stewart urges feminist scholars to "identify women's agency in the midst of social constraint" (Franz and Stewart 21). She recommends that feminist research, in addition to identifying limiting social pressures, also affirm "women's efficacy or control" within these restrictive circumstances (21). Recognizing the choices women have made to resist oppression, even though their methods of agency may be difficult to discern, can lead to a more complete understanding of the ways in which women adapted and lived their lives within limiting social conditions. As suggested by these scholars, private writing offers women agency in situations where they otherwise seem powerless. In reading a journal or diary, we witness a woman in the act of writing, physically placing pen to paper in order to write and give her thoughts a physical and concrete existence. By examining the ways women have used written language, their practice of writing, their personal methods and stylistics, it is possible to comprehend how and why writing worked or, in some cases, did not work effectively to sustain identity and maintain mental equilibrium.

Though it is tempting to think of diaries and journals as full of immediate unedited responses or as the pure and most authentic autobiography, it is important to recognize that writing is not unadulterated thought. More accurately, writing means spinning thought into the potent and empowering web of written language — language styled differently than language used in speech or even immediate thought. As

Margo Culley suggests, like more formal autobiography, these texts are "verbal constructs" in which "the process of selection and arrangement of detail" raises many questions concerning "audience (real or implied), narrative, shape and structure, persona, voice, imagistic and thematic repetition" (*Day at a Time* 10). Similarly, Suzanne Bunkers argues that the diary is "not a shapeless entity; it bears the marks of its writer's examination, selection and shaping of detail" ("What Do Women *Really* Mean?" 215). Indeed diaries are "forms of aesthetic representation through language. . . . They are literature subjectively interpreting life" (Blodgett 5). Examining these writers' "selection and shaping of detail" and their choices of "aesthetic representation" can lead to additional understanding of how women have used writing as a coping device as well as an autobiographical tool. Exploring the writing methods and stylistic choices women have made in their private writings offers scholars insight into the manner in which writing has served to achieve self-understanding and to alleviate isolation. My emphasis will be on the stylistics — particularly textual tools such as thematic repetition — that women have used within their diaries to confront and resist environmental and social constraint.

The creative act of writing is a way of seeking meaning and understanding through the power of language. Lenore Hoffman suggests that there is particular value in viewing women's personal narratives as "works of imagination drawing out themes beyond the limits of their historical specificity" (Hoffman and Culley 1). Though these women wrote privately, usually for themselves or close friends, their creative endeavors reveal their similarities to professional writers "whose most absorbed and passionate hours are spent arranging words on a piece of paper" (Didion 20).

Even for the many women who may not have spent "hours" writing, their lengthy entries prove that they did make the time to write. While journal writing may be an act of self-creation, it is, perhaps more importantly, an act of creation. As Annie Dillard explains, "When you write, you lay out a line of words. The line is a miner's pick, a wood carver's gouge, a surgeon's probe. You wield it and it digs a path you follow. . . . the line of words is a fiber optic, flexible as wire; it illuminates the path just before its fragile tip. You probe with it, delicate as a worm" (3, 7). Using writing to explore her world, a diarist lays out a line of words and reaffirms her mental capabilities. Constructing sentences that create patterns and images with language exercises her intellectual power. In such construction, these women sometimes used writing to find a way through extremely difficult personal circumstances. By writing, these women created something tangible — a record of their thoughts or interpretations of their experiences — out of something intangible — their personal experiences. The sense of accomplishment that comes from filling a blank page with writing certainly seems to have been an experience diarists enjoyed and one which may have been the only weapon they had against otherwise overwhelming situations. Margo Culley argues that these texts offer feminist scholars an opportunity to expand our knowledge of "the human urge to order, structure, create, and communicate meaning" (Hoffman and Culley 16). Just as quilts have become a standard symbol of women's everyday art and their expressions of creativity, women's diaries are similar examples of women's artistic agency. Women's diaries offer us a particularly powerful example of the manner in which women chose to structure their interpretations of their experiences.

Because one of the most significant aspects of diaries is the powerful intimacy these private texts create between the writer and reader, I have chosen to use a personal critical approach. Much recent literary and feminist criticism has begun to encourage the reintroduction of the personal into critical writing. In her polemical essay "Me and My Shadow" (1987), Jane Tompkins argues that the traditional critical voice "insulates academic discourse further from the issues that make feminism matter. That make [women] matter" (24). In the case of diaries and journals, the distancing of academic discourse minimizes one of the most significant aspects of these texts: the intimate portrayal of their writers. Tompkins identifies the power of writers who use the personal within their writing to connect with their audience: "I feel I am being nourished by them, that I'm being allowed to enter a personal relationship with them" (25). The same is often true of reading private diaries and journals. Though as a reader, I may not have been explicitly invited into their private writing, I have entered into a personal relationship with these women, an alliance that is significant to understanding the meaning of their texts. Diane Freedman suggests using the personal critical approach to establish an "aesthetic of familiarity, invitation, emulation, relation — not of postmodern alienation, numbness, surface, coolness" (21). She writes as "part of a community of creative critics" who refuse to "be co-opted by the usual critical conventions of impersonality . . . that [keep] the poetic and personal from the professional and theoretical" (21). Incorporating the poetic and personal into critical writing challenges critics to create a new level of understanding between themselves and their readers. Instead of writing "the kind of writing that does not want to be heard" (10), Marianna

Torgovnik suggests that critics begin to recognize themselves as writers and write "as a person with feelings, histories, and desires — as well as information and knowledge" (10). Whether or not this writing includes autobiographical revelations, Torgovnik continues, "writerly writing is personal writing" that "makes the reader know some things about the writer — a fundamental condition . . . of any real act of communication" (10). Writing to communicate the personal power of these women's diaries and journals is also fundamental to any study that attempts to recognize the significance of this type of private writing for its writers as well as its readers. Francis Murphy Zauhar points to many feminist critics in whose works the personal is used "to create criticism" (116). Creating criticism which communicates the power of these private texts is one of my goals. Rather than alienate readers from these texts, as these women writers frequently have been alienated within culture, I prefer to develop a familiar relationship between myself and my reader — to recognize other critics as readers — that transmits and translates the intimacy these women cultivated in their own writing.

Recognizing the writers within these private texts, their own practices of verbal art, is complicated by the conception of the writer as a public figure as well as a trained professional. In *A Room of One's Own,* Virginia Woolf, having read Dorothy Osborne's letters, remarks: "what a gift that untaught and solitary girl had for the framing of a sentence, for the fashioning of a scene. . . . one could have sworn that she had the makings of a writer in her" (65–66). Succinctly, Woolf identifies the writer as only a public figure, trained to use language to fashion and frame the world. Of course, Osborne *was* a writer, and what she loved to write were letters. We must look at her letters and see *the writer*. Indeed, Woolf challenges her own definitions, reminding herself and her readers: "It would be better, instead of speculating what Mary Carmichael might write and should write, to see what in fact Mary Carmichael did write. . . . For it is useless to say 'Yes, yes, this is very nice; but Jane Austen wrote much better than you do,' when I had to admit that there was no point of likeness between them" (95). Woolf's recommendation to examine what was written rather than what wasn't applies as well to the study and interpretation of diaries and journals. Too often, we see the blanks, the white space, rather than the words, and choose to speculate on what has been left out rather than paying attention to what has been included. As Bunkers argues, we must "recognize and critique our own presuppositions and biases regarding what counts and what doesn't" ("Subjectivity" 119), in order to comprehend women's writing more completely and appreciate the value each woman ascribed to its use. Lensink suggests that "there is not always a correlation between what a diarist writes about and what really matters" (16). She specifically identifies silences on the taboo topics of sexuality and birth control as examples of unspoken issues that "really matter." Rather than viewing these silences as blanks, Bunkers suggests that they be recognized as tools for "encoding" which may "transmit a message in an oblique rather than a direct manner" ("Midwestern Diaries" 194). For Bunkers, encoding may take the form of "indirection, contradiction, deviation and silences" which all become ways "of breaking silences, that is, of finding avenues in which to speak, either directly or indirectly, about what has previously remained unspoken" (194–95). For example, being circumspect about traumatic events, such as the death of a child, allows a woman to speak of them rather than remain silent (194). Indeed, with an attentive reading of women's use of language, we may be able to see how women explain how they felt about writing, marriage, children, and life as well as understand why they chose not to write about what *we* think is so important.

While it is crucial to interpret these silences in diaries, examining what women have written about and how they used writing to explore their lives is equally important. These blank spaces may reveal the failure of writing to explain sufficiently a writer's thoughts. Though the readers may privilege writing as a means of expression and be spurred by curiosity to find out what is missing, the writer herself may find writing about certain subjects dull, unsatisfying, unsuccessful, or inadequate to deal with the subject. If writing about some experiences results in uncontrollable weeping or rage (as in the detailed discussion of the impact of a child's death or violent physical abuse by a spouse), maybe the writer feels it is best not to write at length about these particular experiences. The stark description, the brief entry, the broken-off sentence may be all that is needed to fully describe and relate the writer's response. As Elizabeth Hampsten remarks, "if we are calling [private writing] a literature of omissions, we must wonder why these writings can so affect us while satisfying few of the usual criteria for literary composition" ("Tell Me All You Know" 60). She suggests that what we may read as "callous" may be instead a way to "salvage self-respect and sanity" by starkly describing the event; then, "having described [it], one has no more to say" (60). In this way we can read women on the journey West whose diaries seem filled with burial sightings not as morbidly obsessed with death, but as writing to themselves, "these people have died. I could die. But I am not dead yet. *I am still living.*" After all, every grave a woman can count is a grave she is not in.

We must remember, too, that a journal is not some form of assignment written for critics, but rather a form designed to fulfill the writer's desire to explore her world with writing. When Elizabeth Hampsten writes, "the most effective private chronicles I have been reading do not make a habit of decorative language; they do not play with words or tell jokes or even make metaphorical statements, at least not when they are intently having their say" (*Read This Only to Yourself* 20), my question is, most effective for whom? We need to think about how decorative language, word play, jokes, and metaphorical statements make the writing effective for the writer and allow a writer to have her say. The journal is a form of the writer's own choosing and we must be willing to see these texts as most effective for their writers as well as for their readers. While we seek to understand the place of women in history and society, it is critical that we do not read women for only what we want to hear. We must be willing to "glimpse a past separate from our perceptions of it" (Ezell 9). If our reading is as limited as Gilbert Clandon's, the legacy we receive will be equally limited by our inability to read beyond our expectations. We must also accept that, as in more formal autobiography, the writer is in control of the way she will tell her story. More than any other form, life writing, encumbered as it may be with social and personal constraints, is the story the writer gets to tell. This story of her own choosing reveals "the frameworks of meaning" within which she understands her life (Personal Narratives Group 22).

In this framework of written language, the diary as a singular work, a complete and whole text, offers ample evidence of typical literary concerns. However, the private diary is not constructed as a complete work, but rather as a series of individual entries which serve as independent texts within the larger framework of the diary. As Suzanne Juhasz has noted, "the diary entry . . . is complete in itself; the diary finished when its pages filled. A pattern might emerge, but it will be generated from the significance of the part-in-its-own-right rather than the sought-for whole towards which the part, like arrows, point" ("Some Deep Old Desk" 666). Each work shows us what Germaine Brée terms the "multiplicity of the lived" (175) and "an individual perception of existence translated into words, concrete images, and sequences that show a personality in the process of being in a particular world" (Blodgett 7).

This "process of being" becomes tangible within the powerful episodic structure of the journal. These individual spaces are particular moments of writing, and in reading each we are reading a woman in the very act of writing. Reading these moments is crucial to reading journals as whole texts, even without overall coherence, as well as reading women's *whole* lives. Our reading must take into account the intricacy of this writing act and what Brée terms "the multiplicity of the real" (175). Because the diary is, when we read it, a completed work, it can be comprehended as a whole. However, it is only by recognizing the significance of each individual moment of writing that the larger frame may be understood; conversely, it is in seeing the whole text, the life represented, that the individual moments show their importance. What we read is as complex as the chambered nautilus turning upon itself until its opening. Each curve is marked by shaded coloration as the whole turning forms the external design. Only when it is opened does the shell reveal the internal curl of chambers, one resting on the next in the same curve of the outside — chambers which fill with air to maintain the creature's buoyancy. In this vision of the chambered nautilus is an image of women's diaries. Each diary is in itself a place of transition, a work constructed of individual and independent moments which form the whole text, and a text to be read as a life writing, or more appropriately, a writing life. Just like the shell, the diary must be opened to view the internal chambers, each entry individually a work of transition between the physical and spiritual life of its writer — and each entry a chamber designed to keep its writer afloat. Like the nautilus, these writers maintain their buoyancy not so much because they are continually in danger of drowning, but rather as a structural factor in their living. Their writing is not simply a reaction to their silencing but an action and a moment of agency despite the culture that encourages their passivity.

Opening the diaries of nineteenth-century women and exploring the structural integrity of their writing is critical to understanding how these women have used writing in their lives. My intention here is not to prove how all diaries serve their writers or even how diaries are perfectly suited as the female autobiographical form. What I want to examine is how some individual women used writing to prove their own intellectual power in the face of potentially overwhelming external experiences. Also, I am interested in how their writing reveals the writers' creative agency. In the intimate action of writing, itself a form of thoughtful meditation, these women forged a written space to communicate their spiritual and intellectual strength to themselves as well as to future readers. Analyzing the textual tools each woman used to transmit her own intellectual strength advances the discussion of women's diaries as autobiographical writings by revealing how and why women have employed writing within their lives. By detailing the methods women have applied in their private writing, we can see how women have adapted and expressed creativity and agency in oppressive and traumatic situations. I wish to analyze these texts in detail and observe how women have used their journals to write the juncture between, the merging of, internal and external experience and to explore, figure, detail, construct, and explain their experiences to themselves and future readers. It is in this written space and in the act of writing that the juncture of internal and external life, the meditative moment of self-understanding, is made tangible. It is in this space that we can see how writing helped these women live and how they lived in writing.

Part of discovering how women created meaning for themselves involves reading thoughtfully. Reading these women in the act of writing can be a profound experience. Rita Mae Brown writes that a book is "the most intense, private form of communication between two minds" (ix). These women have left their books — their private and personal communications to themselves — and, intentionally or not, they have been made available to us. The intense communication between the reader and writer of the journal can be alternately deeply moving, horrifying, and amusing. In the act of reading there is a powerful connection between two individuals. As Louise Bernikow begins *Among Women*, it is a moment when "two women are alone in a room" (10). In the act of reading these diaries, I am alone with a woman in *her* book, listening across four generations. She cannot hear me, but I am listening to her. Did she think of such a reader when she lived? Do I think of a future someone reading me? Suzanne Bunkers emphasizes the "self-reflexivity" of her own reading of women's diaries as she accepts and attempts to "understand the ways in which [her] own presuppositions, biases, and hidden agendas might influence" her study of women's journals ("What Do Women *Really* Mean?" 211).

As a diarist, just like Bunkers, I find myself thinking about the nature of reading a woman's diary in connection with my own writing. It is impossible to ignore. In the powerful tangential moments of thought, experience, emotion, action between myself and the woman I'm reading, *her* "line of words fingers [my] own heart. It invades arteries, and enters the heart on a flood of breath" (Dillard 20). Like Silko's Thought-Woman, I am listening to the story she is thinking and I will be telling it. Suddenly the 'progression' of history is a Möbius strip, continually turning inside out and outside in. As Gail Godwin writes: "I have found many sides of myself in the diaries of others. I would like it if I someday reflect future readers to themselves, provide them with examples, courage, and amusement. In these unedited glimpses of the self in other, of others in self, is another one of the covenants posterity makes with the day to day" (15). Like Godwin, when I read a nineteenth-century woman I inevitably imagine someone reading me. This alters my voice much less than it creates a deep sense of respect for and responsibility to the women I am reading. As I hope to be read respectfully, thus I must read with respect. As I hope to be read as an interesting, complex, and whole person, so I must read these women and recognize their complexity. It is no longer possible solely to construct some large and comfortable abstraction about their lives to prove a theoretical position. These women are as real and complex as anyone I know living today. Penelope Franklin writes that "private pages can give us, their readers, permission to be human" (xxviii), and so must we in turn give these writers permission to be human.

When I read a woman's journal, I am reading something in her own hand. Even if the diary is edited or typed from the manuscript, the text began in *her own hand*, not only in the sense of her own handwriting but also her own hand *writing*. When she writes, like Abigail Scott, "I am now seated by a blazing fire," or like Amelia Hadley on top of Independence Rock, "I am now seated on top journalizing," her diary may be more than a century old, but at this moment, this reading, she *is*. When Tennessee Embree writes in the margin of her journal "Beulah made these holes," she *is*. The power of these texts may be in that very simple word: "is." In *her* continuous present, her reality, she is *being*. Just as in Virginia Woolf's "Moments of Being," when Fanny Wilmot suddenly recognizes the human being Julia Craye — "Did Miss Craye actually go to Slater's and buy pins then. . . . Did she stand at the counter like anybody else?" (*Haunted House* 103) — there is the moment of being between writer and reader. It is the point that Juhasz identifies as the moment of true love between mother and infant and between lovers *(Reading from the Heart)*. I would expand this to include the moment of recognition between dear friends. Carefully reading these women's diaries will allow us to see women's interpretations of experience and to recognize these women as well as ourselves. Recognizing the value of these texts as the everyday use of written language offers scholars an opportunity to discover "the fullest possible range of [women's] complexity" (Aptheker 54). The legacy conferred by these texts is one of creative agency, as well as autobiography, and understanding these women's use of writing for themselves, in addition to any particular audience, is necessary to comprehend more completely our heritage. Just as these women used writing as an ordinary practice, it is, as Aptheker suggests, "in the everyday use we make of that heritage in understanding women's lives . . . that the act of knowing from our own experience becomes possible" (54). Recognizing the personal significance of these texts for their writers as well as relating the experience of reading them is integral to comprehending their value as records of women's efficacy and creative agency.

Of course, in the theoretical terrain of postmodernism, any discussion of "identity" or "experience" is fraught with peril. For feminists, the essentializing interpretation of a "women's identity" and a "women's experience," while attractive at some level, is troubling when we consider the various cultural influences on individual "identity" and the conception of "experience." Joan Wallach Scott clearly complicates the unquestioned authenticity of "experience," arguing that taking as "self-evident the identities of those whose experience is being documented" naturalizes difference (25). Rather than analyzing "the workings of [the ideological] system," the emphasis on recovering and relating the experiences of those differentiated within, as well as by, that system, "precludes the workings of this system and of its historicity; instead it reproduces its terms" (Scott 25). It is with this understanding of the complexities of "experience" that I investigate the six women whose diaries are included in this study. Their experiences are clearly influenced by and reflective of the culturally acceptable position of women in the nineteenth-century United States. The experiences available to these women are limited to those expected by their culture, and their own interpretations of experience are similarly influenced. In the case of these women, nineteenth-century expectations for middle-class white women, the cult of true womanhood as well as the earlier conception of republican motherhood, and general cultural attitudes concerning religion, social structure, and racial hierarchy, certainly influenced their own sense of who they were and how they interpreted their experiences.

Coterminous with more intricately defined "experience," the concept of *a* "women's identity" is equally questionable. The theory of an essential "women's identity" rests within the defining discussions of "woman" and gendered "identity." Cultural feminist research, in the effort to valorize women's "undervalued female attributes" advocates the concept of the "essential female" (Alcoff 408). Alcoff clarifies the problems of this approach, suggesting that while the "strengths and attributes" women have developed under oppression "should be correctly credited, valued, and promoted," the essentializing potential of this approach is "in danger of solidifying an important bulwark from sexist oppression: the belief in an innate 'womanhood' to which we must all adhere lest we be deemed either inferior or not 'true' women" (414).

Alcoff also elaborates that alternative approaches, based in French post-structuralist theory, argue that defining "woman" is not possible because in such a defining process we are "duplicating misogynistic strategies when we try to define women, characterize women, or speak for women," and thus "the politics of gender or sexual difference must be replaced with a plurality of difference where gender loses its position of significance" (407). While recognizing the positive attributes of this approach, Alcoff also maintains that "it limits feminism to the negative tactics of reaction and deconstruction and endangers the attack against classical liberalism by discrediting the notion of an epistemologically significant, specific subjectivity" (421). Race, class, and gender are social constructions and are "incapable of decisively validating conceptions of justice and truth because underneath there lies no natural core to build on or liberate or maximize" (421). To alleviate this paradoxical conflict in feminism, Alcoff suggests a concept of "positionality" which takes into consideration Theresa DeLauretis's idea that "the identity of a woman is the product of her own interpretation and reconstruction of her history mediated" through her own cultural contexts (434). Alcoff proposes that this concept discern that "woman"

> is a relational term identifiable only within a (constantly moving) context; but . . . that the position that women find themselves in can be actively utilized (rather than transcended) as a location for the construction of meaning, a place from where meaning is constructed, rather than a place where a meaning can be *discovered* (the meaning of femaleness). The concept of positionality shows how women use their positional perspective as a place from which values are interpreted and constructed rather than the locus of an already determined set of values. (435)

Though the theoretical issues of subjectivity, identity, and the constructed self intrigue feminist theorists, Nancy J. Chodorow and Jane Flax both remind scholars that the theory of the decentered self becomes extremely problematic when applied to actual women. Flax argues, from clinical experience in psychology, that without a "core self . . . the registering of and pleasure in a variety of experiencing (of ourselves, of others, and the outer world) is simply not possible" (93). She points out that this basic cohesion, naively dismissed (she would say) by those who celebrate the "decentered self," makes "the fragmentation of experience something other than a terrifying slide into psychosis" (93). As a case in point she refers to the treatment of a particular client who was forced to confront "the real deficits in her social and intellectual functioning that are the result of having such a fragmented and unintegrated self most of her life" (97). For this real woman, the fragmented self did not "enable [her] to experience and appreciate the flux of existence"(97). Instead, Flax continues, "her relations with people, her internal worlds, and the external world were marked not by an endless dissemination of meanings but rather rigidity, rage, fear, terror, loneliness, self-hate, and a (disavowed but desperate) need for love" (97–98). Thus the freedom to comprehend oneself as "constructed" and "decentered" does not necessarily make the transition from theory to reality particularly well.

Similarly, Chodorow responds to contemporary discussion of gender identity and subjectivity with an emphasis on psychology and clinical evidence. She states a position on gender identity, similar to Alcoff, that takes the complexities of human existence into account. Suggesting a counter argument, Chodorow suggests "that gender cannot be seen as entirely culturally, linguistically, or politically constructed" because of the "individual psychological processes that construct gender for the individual" and create individual meaning (517). She continues, "gender identity or gendered subjectivity — is an inextricable fusion or melding of personally created (emotionally and through unconscious fantasy) and cultural meaning. . . . Individuals thereby create new meanings in terms of their own unique biographies and histories of intrapsychic strategies and practices" (517). Thus even within the culturally acceptable and restrictive models of appropriate gender identity, individual identity still involves personal interpretation and can involve moments of individual agency within that same framework. Chodorow suggests that this personal individuality is "part of the tenacity of gender," and that to "understand and address fully any individual's gender identity requires investigation of a unique confluence of personal and cultural meaning" (524). Allison Weir similarly argues for a concept of self-identity which includes "the capacity to experience oneself as an active and relatively coherent participant in the social world" (185). Weir rightly points out that "the capacity, and responsibility, to problematize and define one's own meaning (one's own identity) is both a burden and privilege of modern subjects. No longer defined by a fixed position in a social system, [she is] relatively free to determine" who she is and who she is going to be (185).

This leads me to the women in my own study who did understand themselves within a fixed social position. Their sense of their own identities incorporated their interpretations of the culturally acceptable role of the "true woman," even as they remained within the parameters of this specific gender identity. What I do not mean to suggest is that these six women all held the same concept of monolithic identity, that there is such a thing as a "women's identity," or that the "core" identity is permanently fixed and unchangeable. Rather, I hope to concentrate on an individual woman's sense of her own identity and the ways she maintained or adapted this sense of her self in her writing — how her writing reveals the flexibility of her own identity. I do think these women, because of their social standing, race, and religious beliefs, had certain cultural conceptions of their identity as women and may have been comforted *as well as* restricted by those definitions. However, the fixity of their own self-conceptions, their own sense of who they think they are or construct themselves to be within their diaries, is questionable. What these diaries reveal, as these women maintain and adapt their sense of their own identities to particular situations, is that their sense of their identity is somewhat under their own personal control. Faced with external circumstances in transition, as in the case of women on the Overland Trail and women during the Civil War, they seek to maintain their individual sense of self because it is the thing over which they have control. When faced with fixed external circumstances, as in the case of the Embrees' abusive husband, these women adapt their identity because it is the thing they can control. Thus their sense of identity is not monolithic or concrete, except when they need it to be. Of course, these nineteenth-century women are restricted in the ways in which they can even conceive themselves to be because of the specific gender expectations of the nineteenth century. They have a limited palette from which to choose the medium for their constructions of identity. However, even with the limitations imposed on these women, they do creatively adapt to their situations using the tools available to them. Like a sonneteer who conforms her words to a restrictive and very specific poetic form, these women still act creatively and individually even within the limited and culturally imposed structure.

The women I have read for this study all chose writing as a form of expression. Some wrote their diaries for eventual known readers; some did not. All found writing a powerful means of expression. The fact that these women wrote diaries at all also indicates a certain level of education and a certain class. Of the six women I discuss, at least one owned slaves and another discusses purchasing diamonds for her daughter who was away at college in another state. This clearly shows the social level of these two women. Of the other diarists, based solely on their stylistic choices, literary allusions to Milton, musical references to Handel, it is clear that they had access to education and valued their literate creativity. In some instances the sheer ability to move from one location to another reveals financial prosperity as well as social mobility. Writing in the nineteenth century also reflected the racial heritage of these women. Though they had differing attitudes toward the issue of slavery, all of these writers were white and were accordingly privileged. They also shared religious convictions, though Jean Rio Baker was a Mormon, describing themselves as Christian and actively participating in church proceedings. All of these aspects of identity and self-definition are taken for granted by these writers but can no longer be taken for granted by scholars. What these women write about and are concerned with, as well as how they define themselves and others, is influenced by these aspects of their lives. Chapter One, "Written into the Landscape: Negotiating Place and Identity in Women's Overland Trail Diaries," discusses two nineteenth-century women who utilized their journals to write through the fear and uncertainty of their westward journey, deriving spiritual strength as they struggled with environmental and personal dislocation and as they confronted the question "who am I if I am not where 'I' have been?" Their detailed representations signify the places they encounter and reveal how their writing enabled each woman to comprehend and successfully negotiate her experiences within the creative framework of language. Chapter Two, "Narratives of Resistance: Negotiating Abuse and the Endangered Self," examines two other nineteenth-century women, married sequentially to the same man, who used their journals to explore their marriages. Both Embrees' writing reveals their altering sense of self as they faced a deeply disturbing pattern of external and internal destruction and asked themselves "who am I if he says I am someone/something different?" Using their writing as a form of resistance to their husband's psychological abuse, each reinforces her own intellectual strength through her writing. Though each maintains the pattern of resistance to her husband's criticism within her diary, her writing eventually becomes inadequate to deal with the external destruction and thus also reveals writing as an insufficient weapon in resisting continued confrontations of a violent nature. Chapter Three, "'When shall this warfare in my soul be ended?': Negotiating Private Conflict and Public Crisis," considers two Confederate women who used their diaries to comprehend their emotional and spiritual responses to the turmoil of the Civil War. Lizzie Hatcher Simons and Cornelia M. Noble use writing to alleviate the psychological pressures they face while their husbands are in combat, asking "who am I if the society and culture in which I have known myself and by whose ideology I have defined my sense of self alters so dramatically that 'I' am no longer recognizable?" Through figurative representation of their emotional struggles, their writing reveals how each engaged her creativity to confront her altering circumstances. Chapter

Four, "Something in Particular: Writing, Journals, and the Evidence of Presence," considers the act of writing as represented within the diaries examined in my study, and discusses the additional impact my study has on the deliberations of the autobiographical significance of women's diaries. To examine as completely as possible how these women used writing, I quote substantial sections of their journals, some of which are unpublished, to reveal how each woman used the act and the process of writing in the particular moment she wrote. I have also maintained the irregular spelling and grammar of these writers to represent their own writing styles accurately. Using the published and well-known diaries of Abigail Jane Scott (Duniway) and Jean Rio Baker, as well as the unpublished typescripts of Henrietta Baker Embree, Tennessee Keys Embree, Cornelia M. Noble, and Elizabeth Hatcher Simons, I will show how these 'ordinary' women writers used the act of writing to make their lives understandable and meaningful, and how their writing reveals their own efforts to maintain, or adapt, their sense of themselves during their written lifetimes.

SHE LEFT NOTHING IN PARTICULAR

ONE

Written into the Landscape

Negotiating Place and Identity in Women's Overland Trail Diaries

Turning slowly, she moved down the walk to the gate, where, far up the road, she could see the white fire of the life-everlasting. The storm and hag-ridden dreams of the night were over, and the land which she had forgotten was waiting to take her back to its heart. Endurance. Fortitude. The spirit of the land was flowing into her, and her own spirit, strengthened and refreshed, was flowing back toward life.

ELLEN GLASGOW, *BARREN GROUND*

West from Houston, the coastal plain of Texas rolls out into green and luxurious hills. It is a landscape that rarely makes it into the movies, and it is the landscape that drew mid-nineteenth-century German immigrants looking for a more peaceful place to live than their war-torn homeland. Small town names mark their migration through the Texas landscape — Frelsburg, New Ulm, Weimer, Schulenburg, New Braunfels, Bracken, Gruene, Boerne, Fredericksburg. The German immigrants settled across a band of south-central Texas and wrote back to their friends and relatives how much the new territory reminded them of home. The significance of these places is most clear in the names that combine the familiar with the unfamiliar — "New" Braunfels and "New" Ulm. This similarity as well as the geographical connection between the new and old places may have eased much of the anxiety produced by the departure from their familiar residence and the arrival in a foreign country. Recognizing this novel space as related to the place they left behind also may have made recognizing themselves in this strange environment much less difficult. Here, they could settle and establish their community much the same as the community they left behind, with the same language, the same friends and relatives, and, most comfortingly, with their own sense of who they were. While these immigrants had most definitely changed places, through their own significations they could assure some constancy to their own sense of identity. However, many travelers journeyed through alien surroundings which held no such comforting personal significance. Encountering territories which were entirely new and frightening challenged immigrants to make these transitional environments understandable through personal and familiar meanings and thus, much less threatening to their own self-understanding. If a writer could comprehend her environment in the same way she had previously been able to do, she could control that which seemed unmanageable and which challenged her own sense of own identity. If a woman could find familiar personal meanings in these new places, she would not have to alter her own sense of who she was and change drastically to discover her place within these different surroundings. Instead she could tailor her surroundings to her own meanings while she remained recognizable to herself, even in very unfamiliar places.

Maria Frawley has noted that leisure travel has been a means for Victorian women to escape the boundaries imposed in their home environment, "getting outside . . . to a place where one could do more" (14). Examining how "writing and travel functioned . . . to enable women to cross physical and ideological boundaries, to expand institutional and psychological borders" (15), Frawley suggests that travel writing reveals how women found "in different places different opportunities for self-fashioning" (37). While the Overland journey[1] certainly influenced their identities as Victorian women, unlike women who traveled for leisure, the women on the Overland Trail departed from familiar places to which they would not return. They faced the uncertainty of how their own sense of themselves and their own understanding of their identities would be threatened or drastically altered as they left the places they had known and where they had previously been known. While these women might re-fashion their identities in the process of traveling, they were without the assurance that their own sense of who they were, which was intertwined with their

4

previous home/place, would not alter beyond recognition. How could they maintain a sense of who they were while the journey took them away from the places they knew and people who they had known themselves to be? Would their identities alter as much as the terrain through which they traveled? Unlike the Victorian women travelers Frawley discusses, who were reassured "that their status as English . . . women would guarantee a privileged position abroad" and were able to write from a "privileged perspective [which] enabled them to experience and record with great confidence" (20), women on the Overland Trail were confronted with potential loss of identity as they left behind any comforting social class and privileged status related to their position in a particular place. They would also be traveling through land which was not even a recognizable place, named only by the vague and nebulous term "territory." Would their own social status *really* matter without the society in which it was formed? Of course, one of the powerful attractions of the frontier was the opportunity it offered many to escape from certain restrictive class structures. While this was certainly comforting to women who were striving to leave poverty behind and to grow rich on the frontier, others may have been less than thrilled with the potential loss of social position, especially if a significant portion of a woman's self-understanding — the way she understood herself to be — was derived from her social position within her community and from the actual domestic space of her home. Leaving these well-known regions, how would she know herself and the "who" she had been in these places?

Though women's frontier diaries have offered scholars the opportunity to examine women's "experience" of the westward expansion, the diaries kept by women on the

Overland Trail differ from those maintained by women who were settled on the frontier, established their homes in one particular place, and replicated the domestic places they had left as closely as possible. Lillian Schlissel notes that Overland diaries were "a special kind of diary" meant for publication or for relatives who intended to make the journey at a later date (11). In addition, these Overland diaries were maintained during a physical transition. As women traveled away from their known environments, they negotiated the psychological modifications of their identity — their sense of who they were — which had been formed in a familiar and particular place and which was now challenged by the new environments through which they traveled. The journey itself aided women in these identity transitions, as Sandra Myres suggests, because "lessons of flexibility and adaptability" learned on the trail "helped women cope with the new conditions and new problems" of life on the frontier (139).

As these women traveled through the unfamiliar regions of the Overland Trail, the literal space between their former homes and their new homes, as well as the figurative space between who they once were and who they would now become, also had to be safely traversed. To do so, they began to imbue these new places with familiar meaning in an effort to adapt to the changes induced by the journey. As Delys Bird argues of women in colonial Australia, "the effort to speak the landscape . . . figures the effort to adapt and to familiarize" life in a distant colonial state (22). This effort to speak the "landscape" involves a certain cultural understanding of how places are appropriately perceived. Barbara Bender points out that "we 'perceive' landscapes." In doing so, "we are the point from which the 'seeing' occurs," and thus, the description is an "ego-centered landscape, a perspectival landscape, a landscape of views and vistas" (1). Accordingly these landscapes must be "contextualized," because they depend on factors such as gender, age, class, caste, and social and economic conditions. People's landscapes also use "different spatial scales . . . horizontally across the surface of the world, or vertically — up to the heavens, down to the depths" and "different temporal scales, engaging with the past and with the future in many different ways" (2). Bender argues this engagement may sometimes "be very conscious — a way of laying claims, of justifying and legitimating a particular place in the world" or "sometimes almost unconscious — part of the routine of everyday existence" (2). Of course, the nineteenth-century women describing the landscapes they encountered on the Overland Trail were influenced by traditional and specific Western landscape aesthetics. My intention here is not to examine these diaries for the use of these aesthetics or to explain the history of landscapes.[2] However, it is significant to understand that these writers did not write without influence or create "pure" descriptions in their landscapes. In fact, I suggest that these very familiar aesthetics and descriptive patterns enabled these women to recognize otherwise unfamiliar spaces. Thus, they made these places knowable through the use of the comforting terms and descriptions which reflected their own sensibilities. Even so, European aesthetics could not adequately be applied to some of the terrain in the far Western United States. Indeed, "the strange, but undeniably spectacular sights of the Far West forced Americans to come up with new standards and descriptive strategies independent from powerful European ideas" (Hyde 9). Hyde argues that this process of "grappling with a language suitable to the realities of the Far

Western landscape helped forge a particularly American culture" (9). Integrating early nineteenth-century East Coast conceptions of landscape significance with "the new concepts of beauty and value forged in the West" during the last half of the century, "the struggle to interpret far Western landscape had given Americans the seed of an independent culture" (9). In these Overland Trail diaries we see the beginning of this process as well as the process by which these women made this new territory recognizable and less threatening to their own sense of themselves.

The natural surroundings figure prominently in women's Overland diaries; John Mack Faragher identifies "the natural beauty of the landscape" as one of the three major themes within both men's and women's Overland diaries (12). Martha Mitten Allen also notes the eloquence of women's landscape description, particularly the "romantic rhetoric" at which women "excelled" (56). As a convention of travel writing, such landscape description, scholars have suggested, reflects the colonizing impulse, an attempt to own the land through language. Mary Louise Pratt suggests that the panoramic view common in travel writing represents a "fantasy of dominance" (124) in which the "eye *knows itself* to be looking at prospects in the temporal sense — as possibilities for the future, resources to be developed, landscapes to be peopled or repeopled by Europeans" (125; original emphasis). Thus, as Sara Mills writes, "in the physical act of describing the landscape, the narrator is also mastering it" (78). Mills suggests that in Pratt's interpretation, the "narrator who includes a panoramic scene arrogates to herself the power of the colonial position" (79). Thus, by describing the landscape before her, a woman claims ownership through language and asserts her influence on the landscape. I suggest she also makes the unfamiliar territory more psychologically manageable through her own personal significations. If she recognizes the land before her as familiar and can label it so, it will be much less incomprehensible and much less threatening to her sense of who she is and who she knows herself to be — the "who" she was in her previous place. The unknown space becomes a known place and she herself can remain familiar and unthreatened by her new environment.

Annette Kolodny argues in *The Land Before Her* that women have "in the process of projecting symbolic contents onto otherwise unknown terrains . . . made those terrains their own" (xii). Kolodny's study maintains that women viewed the landscape through the lens of ownership and "dreamed of transforming the wilderness," claiming "the frontiers as a potential sanctuary for an idealized domesticity" (xii-xiii). Thus, women viewed the American frontier with a sense of responsibility and an understanding of their own role in transforming the landscape through their colonizing of it. In addition to the colonizing impulse evident in landscape description, Mills argues, the narrator of a travel text also attempts to identify with the places and people she depicts to "distinguish" herself from other travelers, establish the authenticity of her account, and to reveal her position of intimacy, which "gives her the authority to describe" (80). Thus, through these portrayals, a writer also identifies her own ability to adapt and to become a part of the land she visits. By identifying "with" these new places, she discovers her familiar self in foreign spaces.

Similarly, in the Overland diaries, women had to adapt to new spaces and discover a way to become part of these new places without becoming entirely foreign to themselves. However, they were not the same kind of traveler that Mills,

Pratt, or Kolodny describe. As they viewed land that they would not settle, an environment that they would only pass through, these women had to establish their connection to these places in different terms. Rather than viewing their relationship to the land in terms of their impact on their surroundings, these women wrote themselves into the landscape, defining and making familiar the territories which threatened their own sense of identity as they attempted to comprehend the personal influence of the transitional space/place. As Gayle Davis suggests, one function of the frontier diary was to mediate between the "author's self-perception as a Victorian lady and her feared loss of that identity in the wild" (7). During their Overland travel through the American frontier, these women, fortified by their writing, located themselves through their imagistic descriptions of these transitional places, just as they had been positioned within the particular places they had previously known. Using description to identify, solidify, and know these transitional landscapes, these writers reinforced their own identities as they moved between old and new territories, and negotiated the transitions between the familiar and unfamiliar by applying customary interpretations of their new surroundings. As external circumstances altered rather dramatically, these women reinforced and controlled their own sense of self in their writing as they signified the land through which they journeyed. Thus, while they could not control the places they encountered, they could control their interpretations and could maintain a comforting familiarity with these places as well as their own sense of identity.

Seventeen-year-old Abigail Jane Scott, "Jenny," traveled with her family to Oregon in 1852.[3] After the Missouri Compromise of 1850, Tucker Scott and his relatives, all

Free-Soilers, made the decision to leave for Oregon, a "sanctuary from the evil effects of slavery . . . where one could be prosperous, healthy and free" (Moynihan 28). Self-educated, politically conscious, and fervently religious, Tucker Scott moved his entire family west to Oregon. Jenny, who would eventually become one of the West's famous suffragists (Abigail Jane Scott Duniway), was charged with keeping the family diary "correct" as it was most likely intended for future publication (31). Jenny also wrote for herself. In her elaborate descriptions, her education and political ideology are apparent. While not wealthy, the Scotts were most certainly middle class and also considered themselves anti-slavery. In her descriptions, Scott reiterates her familiar and emotional relationship with the land through which she travels, despite her inexperience with the new environment, and her details reflect her personal self-understanding as well as the cultural perspective from which she wrote.

One year previous, in 1851, Jean Rio Baker, a Mormon traveling from England, carefully observes her sea voyage, her experience in New Orleans, and her Overland trip to Utah. A widow, forty-year-old Baker departed England January 4, 1851; arrived at New Orleans March 20; traveled up the Mississippi to eastern Iowa, then across the Great Plains to Salt Lake City, where she arrived approximately nine months after having left England (Baker 203-4). The edition of her diary I have used includes scant information concerning her economic or political ideology or her education; however, it is clear in her diary that Baker was highly educated and very devout. Her references to Handel's Chronicles, Milton's *Paradise Lost*, and other literary works as well as her articulate and detailed descriptions of her surroundings clearly indicate her social class and education level. Baker details her landscapes with religious imagery that fortifies her spiritual identity through the evidence of divine creation. Both women were certainly influenced by European landscape aesthetics and practice this visual approach when they describe their surroundings. Whether the landscapes described are the prairie, the peaks of the Rocky Mountains, or even the cities, these women's elaborate, as well as stark, versions of the landscapes they encountered detail their attempts to keep their sense of themselves as they traveled out of place. The identity questions these women may have been asking themselves were "how do I know me when I am not where I have been? How do I remain recognizable to myself as the places surrounding me become increasingly unrecognizable? Who am I if I do not know the where in which I am?" What they may have been trying to answer was "no matter *where* I go, there *I* am." Describing the unfamiliar spaces with familiar terminology and personal significance, both Scott and Baker make their surroundings recognizable and find themselves in place.

Jenny Scott traveled with her large family and many other relatives who made up the wagon train bound for Oregon.[4] Her immediate family consisted of John Tucker Scott, 43; Ann Scott, 40; Fanny, 19; Jenny, 17; Maggie, 15; Harvey, 14; Catherine (Kit), 13; Etty, 11; Henry, 9; Maria, 5; and Willie, 3. There were thirty-six additional relatives, friends, and travel companions in their train (Scott 32–38). The Scott family departed Illinois April 2, 1852, and arrived at French Prairie, Oregon, between September 29 and October 1, 1852. The six-month journey took the party from Tazewell County, Illinois, to Quincy, Illinois; St. Joseph's, Missouri; Fort Kearney, Nebraska; up the Platte River to

Fort Laramie, Wyoming; then through the South Pass and on southwest of the Grand Tetons to the Snake River. The last portion of the trip followed the Snake River, then they crossed the Blue Mountains and the Grande Ronde Valley to the Columbia River, near The Dalles. The final section was over the Cascades to the Willamette Valley (Moynihan 29).

On April 2, 1852, Jenny opens the diary with an entry briefly detailing the family's departure from their familiar home in Illinois, "leaving home, home friends and home associates in Old Tazewell" (39). She remarks that they have had "no trouble at all except what has been occasioned by bidding farewell forever to those with whom most of us have associated all our lives" (39). Everything in Scott's description here elaborates the significance of Tazewell County. She leaves "home, home friends and home associates" with whom she and her family have been "associated all [their] lives." Explaining her departure from the only place she has known and has been known, Scott begins almost immediately a pattern of detailed description, which she maintains throughout her journal and through which she makes the new places she sees identifiable. Applying this strategy to manage her increasing sense of dislocation, Scott describes these new territories with familiar terms, drawing heavily on the conventional Romantic imagery which links God and nature. As Sandra Myres notes, these pioneer writers were "particularly influenced by the romanticism of the age" and "exalted nature and pondered the religious significance of the natural wonders they encountered" (30). As Scott confronts the changing imagery before her, she employs the familiar romantic interpretations to mediate her responses to these unfamiliar areas. Constructing the scenery with these conventional descriptors, Scott is able to familiarize her surroundings and thus render the landscape as a reassuring reminder of her previous home. In recalling the landscape where she "was wont to roam oer hill and dale" and where she "loved to silently muse over the varying vicissitudes of life and loved to wander alone to the sequestered grove, to hold communion unseen by mortal eye with the works of nature and of God" (39), Scott details her connection with the natural surroundings, bolstering her sense of identity by reminding herself of her previous intimate association with the land as she faces a new landscape. If she can remember how the land has previously been comforting and has been a significant indicator of a divine presence, she can face the new spaces which will continue to indicate the presence of a familiar God, and her own interpretation will reinforce what she has known to be previously true about the environment. Thus, the land is not new and challenging to her sense of who she is but rather it is more of the landscape she has previously enjoyed and a place where she will be equally recognizable.

As Annette Kolodny has suggested of other women pioneers, Scott views her landscape as a garden paradise, a "sequestered grove" where she is able to hold "communion" with God and nature. Establishing her connection to this garden place, Scott copes with her departure from the familiar by using her previous experience of the environment to illuminate her new condition. Even if this place is entirely new, Scott strives to adapt to the changes she experiences by her comfortingly familiar interpretations. She writes, "I am seated by a blazing fire with Heavens canopy over my head trying to compose my mind" (39). Composing her vivid imagery also seems to compose her mind as she writes eloquently of the images surrounding her as well as those she left, thus fusing old and new, familiar and strange, in her description. Still, like the fire before her, she seems "flickering and uncertain" as she tries "almost in vain . . . [to] form her thoughts into writing" (40). Seemingly unable to express her emotional state, her vivid description is the tactic she employs to cope with her new experiences. By applying her own familiar interpretations to the new places she encounters, Scott is able to identify the environment and identify with her surroundings. Though she is out of place, she engages description to situate herself within the strange environment, just as she had previously identified herself within the familiar landscape of her home. Thus she makes this space a familiar place. As Davis has suggested, Scott writes to mediate between the areas she departs and the regions she now encounters, enabling her to form the scenery with her own representations and to make the new regions recognizable.

Scott continues to employ this strategy throughout her journal. When the Scott family crosses the Mississippi on April 14 and finally leaves Illinois, Scott recalls the comfort of her remembered landscape as she contemplates her psychological and physical crossing:

> while I am now writing we are launched on the great bosom of the great Father of Waters bound for a landing place and while I look with a feeling of calm contentment upon the placid current of this great river, I at the same time think with feelings which defy description of the loved home of my childhood, my native state; Safely landed and encamped for the night upon the Missouri side. (43)

Thinking of her final departure from her home state triggers powerful emotions for Scott. Though her image of "the great bosom of the great Father of Waters" seems spiritually comforting, her "calm contentment" is countered by her feelings which "defy description," and she breaks off from writing. While she has previously elaborated on her description, her lack of detail expresses her anxiety here. Entering this new landscape and crossing the physical boundary between the familiar and unfamiliar, she recalls her previous home and contemplates the transition from her "native" state of being to her new, dislocated state. Scott considers her physical shift from her "loved home" as well as her personal changes from "childhood" to her present, seventeen-year-old self. As she travels, she must adapt not only to the new environments but also to the changes in her childhood identity, which is linked so closely with her native state. When she closes her entry, her form shifts from prose to poetry as she attempts to articulate her emotions while she thinks of her departure: "Old Illinois I say farewell / Tho long in thee I'd love to dwell / Yet I must go perhaps no more / To reach this lovely land and shore" (43). Again she reminisces about her place within the landscape she leaves. Delys Bird suggests the new landscape "becomes emblematic of the loss suffered by the emigrant" and provokes a visual and verbal crisis that makes that landscape inexpressible (22). In Scott's poetic construction, she identifies her loss and reinforces her emotional association with the landscape. She copes with this verbal crisis by applying the form and language of poetry rather than her own, more personal prose, as she faces the inexpressible landscape on the Mississippi's western shore.

As Scott journeys further west across Missouri, her earthly paradise is despoiled by human habitation, and the landscape which proved so comforting earlier is marked with corrupting influences. From April 15 through April 26, Jenny is occupied with the discomforting Missouri scenery. She writes briefly about the illness within the wagon train, her distaste for slavery she sees — "slavery is a withering blight upon the prospects, happiness, and freedom of Our Nation" (44)[5] — and the economic dangers of the journey: "A sharper tried to make us pay $10 for the privilege of grazing cattle on a piece of prairie land near his dwelling but we knew what we were about and saved our money" (46). Only after the family passes through this disagreeable region does Scott detail some of the landscape she encountered. Her descriptions also reflect her feelings about the last two weeks of travel. The previous landscape "almost without single exception looked entirely unfit for the abode of men or women" (47). This landscape offered "no signs of civilization worth mentioning — in fact nothing at all" except the occasional "shabby log hut which exactly corresponded to the destitute and desolate scenery around us" (47). In the alienating scenery of Missouri, Scott's descriptions reinforce her own ideology and her family's ability to maintain their sense of identity in what Jenny describes as the socially backward environment. As she details the landscape that looks "more and more like civilization," she reinforces her own identity as a "civilized" traveler (47). Differentiating herself from the inhabitants of Missouri, Scott illustrates the strength of her own character by the contrast with the "sharpers" and slave traders of Missouri. Unlike her previous descriptions, she finds no place for herself within this landscape. In this case, the landscape is not even worthy of her presence. Kolodny describes a similar pattern in Margaret Fuller's *Summer on the Lakes,* noting confrontation between Fuller's idyllic vision of the frontier and the reality of life there. While Fuller "wanted to see settlement without despoliation" (116), she found the typical frontier home became a place of "domestic captivity" (130). By April 30, Scott can compare the desolate landscape, filled with slave owners and sharpers, with the prairie landscape that looks "more and more like civilization" (47) — a familiar place where Scott is more *at home*.

As Scott faces an entirely new landscape, she attempts to make the environment more familiar by using conventional nineteenth-century aesthetic terminology: "We are now rolling over a splendid looking prairie while blue tinged timber in the distance, the wild flowers and shrubs beneath our feet and the numerous herds conteantedly grazing near us presents an appearance at once picturesque and sublime" (47). This beautiful pastoral scene, which looks "more and more like civilization" is, interestingly, without people or evidence of human habitation. Instead, the natural world is what is most civilized, rather than the previous inhabited landscape which contained "no signs of civilization." In this unpeopled place, Scott can manipulate the description to suit her needs. She can reinforce her sense of identity, her own civilized "nature," without having to confront other people who directly challenge her sense of self. While she used the people of Missouri to affirm her sense of self by firmly opposing their pro-slavery position, here she can recognize herself with less effort. Delys Bird argues that referencing the landscape with the familiar terms picturesque and sublime "exemplifies the strangeness [in the landscape] . . . which women struggled to articulate" (28). By employing these conventional terms of landscape description, women were "able to displace or deny that strangeness," bring the landscape "under their linguistic and cultural control," and begin the "process of demystification" (28). Thus, as Scott departs a spoiled landscape and enters an equally unfamiliar environment, she returns to conventional descriptive terms to reconnect with the scenes she describes. While Missouri was certainly disquieting, Scott was able to enforce her own sense of self by reiterating her political opposition to the state's slave status. Here she must apply these conventional descriptors to demystify the prairie landscape and identify her intimate connection with the natural world.

As the family continues their journey, the dangers become more apparent, and Scott's descriptions continue to show her attempts to deal with these problems and her own fear. When, in the span of two days, her family passes seven graves and another family burying their son in the "ocean like and seemingly boundless plains" (50), Scott turns to the comforting landscape beyond these lethal images. She writes, "the *plains* certainly wear a charm which I little expected to see" and have "a brilliancy which certainly cannot be surpassed in any country or in any prairie" (51; original emphasis). Identifying the "charm" and "brilliancy" of the countryside, Scott expresses her delight in the scenic beauty. While she did not seem to have any expectations for this place, she happily applies the language which makes the alien prairie familiar. Though this is an entirely new landscape, her descriptions preserve the continuity of her interpretations and reflect her attempts to maintain her familiar identity as she encounters more gruesome images. Amidst the scenes of death that the family has passed, Scott is able to avoid the destructive and fearful imagery she faces by finding the natural beauty of the environment. In her entry dated May 14, she explains: "by going off the main road a little one can see a sight which looks fit for angels to admire;

The little hollows which at a short distance from the road we can see almost anytime are generally filled with flowers and variegated with ten thousand which are almost sufficient to perfectly enchant the mind of every lover of nature" (51). Since the main road is lined with graves and offers a constant grim reminder of death, Scott finds her solace in observing nature "off" the main road, which is "almost sufficient" to help her forget the other images she sees. Julie Roy Jeffrey argues that the continued references to flowers in women's diaries "connected many women to the remembered world of their flower gardens — landscapes that were cultivated, fertile and familiar" (72). Similarly, Scott is able to make the horrible surroundings beautiful as well as linguistically and personally manageable. Rather than focus on the strange and death-filled images on the main road, Scott can retreat and find a comforting and familiar place to reinstate her own significance and her interpretations. She makes her own place in the territory, reiterating her love of nature against the other horrors she views. Striving to deal with her fear and anxiety, she turns to writing about the living landscape.

In this environment hostile to human life, Scott contin-ues to reinforce her significance and maintain her sense of her identity by drawing on the same Romantic imagery she applied earlier in her journal. By observing the natural world and the human beings within it, Scott makes her connection to the landscape clear. On June 3, eighteen days after her entry on the beautiful prairie, Scott again expounds on the "romantic spectacle" (60) she sees before her. After three weeks marked by the grave-lined trail, the Scotts watch more members of their train falling ill, discover the unearthed body of a man stabbed to death with a Bowie knife, and encoun-ter another Illinois family turning back for the States. Scott escapes the frightening environment briefly by riding up to the bluffs above the Platte River. Her description indicates the comfort she finds there as she describes the infinitesimal human drama encompassed by the natural world. With the Platte "flowing in peaceful music" below her, Scott views, on one side of the bluff, "the emigrants wagons cattle and horses on the road in either direction as far as the eye could reach" (60). Scott writes, this "living mass . . . contrasted so strangely with the other side . . . where I was" (60). As opposed to the living mass of emigrants, Scott identifies herself with the "other side" — the more natural, the more civilized, location. She does not identify with the other emigrants but places herself within gardenlike surroundings which she contrasts to the trail. Again she goes off the main road to alleviate the stresses of her journey. This comparative description is similar to her response to the Missouri landscape, where she identified the natural world as far more civilized than the landscapes human beings had created, or ruined. As she had previously removed herself psychologically from the dangers and trauma of the trail, Scott again chooses flower and garden imagery to describe the landscape with which she prefers to identify. She continues her panorama: "the ground was in most places almost covered with a kind of flower the seed of which exactly resembles our buck-wheat while the flower in shape, size and color exactly resembles the common touch-me-not" (60). As on her journey through Missouri and the miserable environment she found there, Scott finds herself much more comfortable with the natural world than with other emigrants on this journey. In her most stressful moments, Scott turns to nature and the minute details of the flowers she finds. As she reminds herself of the ways in which she always views flowers, she finds her own self equally familiar. In her writing, Scott seems to remind herself that she knows who she is through the ways she has always seen. Thus as she writes and sees familiar flowers, she remains recognizable to herself. Like Georgia O'Keeffe, who remarked, "when you take a flower in your hand and really look at it, it's your world for a moment" (Robinson 279), Scott sees flowers and writes this world. In her descriptions of flowers, she is able to refocus, shifting the horrors of her journey and "the living mass of emigrants" to find beauty in the miniature landscape of the flower.

When Jenny's mother, Ann Scott, dies of cholera, Scott writes poignantly of the landscape where her mother is buried and once again finds the beauty of the natural world a means to comprehend the horror of her loss. Having just recovered from cholera herself, Scott resumes writing June 20, returning to the journal which was maintained by her sister Maggie during this illness.[6] She records her mother's death with spiritual language appropriate for the family's loss and recognition of their own powerlessness in the face of a greater power: "How mysterious are the works of an all wise and overruling Providence! We little thought while last Sabbath's pleasant sun shed upon us his congenial rays that when the next should come it would find us mourning over the sickness and death of our beloved Mother!" (71). This tragedy seems an ordering of "Providence" and Jenny wearily notes that the family's best efforts to save Ann Scott are insufficient: "her constitution long impaired by disease was unable to withstand the attack and this afternoon . . . her wearied spirit took its flight and then we realized we were bereaved indeed" (71).

In her struggle to comprehend this affliction, Scott details the landscape surrounding the grave, hoping to be able find it if they ever returned. According to Duniway's biography, they were never able to locate the grave that had been chiseled in sandstone and covered with stones (Moynihan 36). For Scott, her mother's gravesite is "a romantic one" and perfectly suited "for the last resting place of a lover of rural scenery such as she was [and] when in good health always delighted in" (71). Scott commits to paper as well as her memory a precise and beautiful description of this scenery as she mourns her loss:

> The grave is situated on an eminence which overlooks a ravine intersected with groves of small pine and cedar trees; In about the centre of this ravine or rather basin, there wells a spring of icy coldness, clear as crystal. . . . In the outskirts of this basin clusters of wild roses and various other wild flowers grow in abundance.;: And from an eminence where all this can be viewed at a single glance, reposes the last earthly remains of *my mother*. (71–72; original emphasis)

This landscape contrasts distinctly with the previous descriptions of other burials on the lonely uninhabited and desolate plains as Scott details carefully the beautiful environment of her mother's grave. Confronted with the loss of her mother, Scott describes the "clusters of wild roses" as well as the "small pine and cedar trees" which can all be seen from her mother's grave. As in her previous confrontations with death and disease, Scott writes for the strength and the comfort she has found earlier in the natural world. Her detailed description identifies the landscape surrounding her mother's grave and establishes this place as one of garden-like and memorable romantic beauty. Again Scott emphasizes her connection to nature in this description; however, in this instance, she does not describe any divine presence. Instead she is now tied to this landscape by her relationship to her own mother. Rather than articulating the abstract relationship between herself and God, this description emphasizes her relationship with her mother. Slowly her "communion" with God seems to deteriorate as she confronts less-than-divine events.

After departing from this site, Scott continues to detail her surroundings, rather than any internal turmoil she feels. As when she left her home, her painful emotions cannot be expressed, and she describes on June 22, the day following her mother's burial, what she sees: "the rocky cliffs resemble rude images of men and animals, rising up as if to mock the surrounding sterile and barren scenery" (73). This description contrasts sharply with the beauty of her mother's grave and reflects not only the "sterile" and mocking cliffs, but also may indicate her own state of despair and isolation. As in the description of her mother's gravesite, she does not see any divinity within these places, only "rude images" which seem to rise up "to mock the surrounding sterile and barren scenery" of eastern Wyoming. Now, her descriptions seem to reflect her own anger and fear, and she seems to place herself in these descriptions just as she had done in more peaceful places. While her landscapes have previously mirrored her connection with God and emphasized the beauty of the natural environment, her descriptions here seem to mirror a version of God who seems quite distant. She no longer makes an effort to see her connection with God through the landscape. Now, as in Missouri, the landscape seems hostile to her own sense of her identity even as her descriptions reflect her own bitterness. Three days and thirteen grave sightings later, she returns to the pattern of description which does include continued references to her surroundings' beauty. However, she does not immediately reintegrate the references to God which had previously seemed comforting. As she has done earlier, Scott begins to describe the beauty rather than the horror before her. In the "very grand and altogether romantic view" of the bluffs surrounding the river, Scott finds "a city of dome shaped houses, churches and every manner of public buildings" which have an "imposing appearance on account of being surrounded by an impenetrable looking fortress" (75). Notably, at the close of this entry, she writes, "passed no new graves" (75). Only when the lethal images subside can Scott return to the comforting descriptions which she has previously employed. Still her descriptions differ significantly from her previously peaceful and garden-like images. These images do not suffice to explain clearly the scenery encounters along the Platte River.

By June 29, approximately one month after her mother's death, Scott returns to describing the natural environment, reflecting on her sorrow and finding comfort in the place she portrays. Perhaps more psychologically as well as physically distanced from the event, Scott can again ponder her surroundings and reinforce her sense of her identity through her writing. As in her earliest entries, her writing reveals the personal significance of the space she inhabits. Situating her writing moment clearly, she expresses the significance of a literal and figurative place, writing "I am now seated on the bank of the river upon a ledge of rocks which forms a kind of natural sofa" (99). In this comfortingly domestic environment, she continues to detail the scenery as "of a truly wild and romantic description" with "huge piles of rock ris[ing] up in bold array around me with often a cedar nodding at their tops" (100). After she describes her immediate surroundings, she begins to see it as a reminder of her own emotional conflicts. Like her very first entry, she links the remembered landscape of her home to the horizon before her:

> Off in a northeastern direction from me a seeming-less endless sage plain is situated and when I look with admiration upon this wild plain and reflect that far, far beyond it is the home of my childhood together with dear relatives and friends whose faces I perchance may never behold again, a feeling arises in my breast of peaceful sadness which may be imagined but not described. (100)

As her previous descriptions of the landscape when her emotions become too painful, Scott ends her entry, perhaps unable to write what she feels most deeply. The "peaceful sadness" is broken by the next day's disaster. A cattle stampede across the swift Snake River results in the death of John McDonald,[7] "a worthy young man" who had "won the esteem of all" (101). As well as his death, the family suffers the loss of a favorite horse and injury of other members of the group. Scott's description of her environment relates her chaotic feelings. Writing "seated in the same place where I was writing last evening," Scott relates how her interpretations of the previously peaceful landscape have been changed by this incident. The sound of the river is "no longer pleasant music, but a jarring discordant sound." She cannot meditate quietly; instead she writes: "I startle and half rise to my feet at the rustling of the leaves about me; and these huge rocks which I then looked upon with admiration, now only terrify as I have thought several times when I would hastily glance around me that a wily Indian or a wild beast was in readiness to destroy me, but I still love this spot as It corresponds with my feelings" (102). While Scott had previously found herself comforted by the domestic familiarity of this place, she now describes it with distinctly different imagery. Now she focuses on the wildly terrifying surroundings which "correspond" to her feelings following McDonald's death. While she needed comfort earlier and found it with her descriptions of the romantic and domestic space, she now locates her frantic emotions with the corroborating interpretations. Clearly, no matter what it looks like, this place can be made to reflect whatever Scott needs it to. Just as in her previous landscapes, Scott makes this place known to herself through her own interpretations of it. Here is the where in which Scott can place herself, seeing her own sense of self in the corresponding imagery. Scott's writings echo Margaret Fuller's description of Niagara Falls in *Summer on the Lakes* (1843). Just as Scott notes the power of the river and her wariness, Fuller writes, "the perpetual trampling of the waters seized my senses. I felt that no other sound, however near could be heard and would start and look behind me for a foe" (Fuller 72). Like Scott, who sits on the "natural sofa" to contemplate her surroundings, Fuller "liked best . . . to sit on Table Rock, close to the great fall. There all power of observing details, all separate consciousness, was quite lost" (72). As she struggles to overcome the catastrophe she has experienced, Scott seeks Fuller's ability to lose her "separate consciousness." Surrounded by the powerful and overwhelming environment, she does not, or cannot, think of her losses. While she previously described the flowers and other details of the landscape to distract herself from the dangers of her journey, she desires complete distraction in an environment which seems much more powerful than herself and yet is as powerful as her own emotions. Surrounded by the roaring water, she finds the environment empathetic to her feelings.

Scott seeks this complete distraction again August 27, approximately two months later, in writing the detailed description of her surroundings while her four-year-old brother Willie is deathly ill with "cholera infantum." As her family watches his decline over "the last 96 hours," Scott seeks comfort in the natural world, describing the "excellent springs and beautiful spring branches" (116). She lists the trees which line the stream, "alder birch, bitter Cottonwood and balm of Gilead" and closes her entry by painfully expressing her hopelessness: "our little Willie lingered through the day . . . but he is so debilitated that he cannot live much longer" (116). In her entry of the following day she records Willie's death and, like her entry on the death and burial of her mother, Scott carefully describes the landscape, detailing this scenery as she did the surroundings of her mother's grave. Scott notes her brother's grave is situated "upon an elevated plain in a spot of sweet seclusion" (117). She constructs the garden around his grave, writing: "a beautiful cedar waves its wide spread branches over his tomb, and here beneath its shade I have wandered in remote seclusion to be alone with Willie and his God and while I reflect that he is now beyond the reach of mortal suffering, in my heart I praise the Lord, who gave and who has taken away" (117). The beautiful cedar tree years later recalled as the "only living thing," was still living some "twenty years later" (117n) when a family member returned to the spot. Scott draws on the romantic imagery linking herself with God and nature and reassures herself of her own position within the landscape and the comfort she finds there. Though she refers to "Willie and his God" in her entry, she closes with her own prayer through which she seems to remind herself of her own faith: "in my heart I praise the Lord, who gave and who has taken away." Writing of this tree and its comforting presence, Scott can remember the tree rather than the horrifying death of her little brother. As Sethe, in Toni Morrison's *Beloved*, recalls Sweet Home's horror "hidden in lacy groves" of the "most beautiful sycamores in the world" and remembers "the wonderful soughing trees rather than the boys" hanging in them (Morrison 6), Scott turns to the tree, describing the only beautiful thing she is able to see.

Scott continues writing for another month until the family reaches Oregon and her entries are interspersed with entries written by her father and sister. For Scott, the landscape continues to distract her from the traumas she endures. Clearly throughout her journal, she has found beauty and comfort in the landscape, even when this beauty seems extremely difficult to see. Writing and thinking about the landscape surrounding her, Scott can endure the misery and death she encounters even if she is unable to understand it. As Ellen Glasgow writes of post–World War I England, "all this beauty . . . we had forgotten there was all this beauty in the world" (*Woman Within* 252). Instead of thinking only of the horror, by writing of the landscape, Scott reminds herself of all the beauty, even if it is small and, at times, very difficult to find. Despite the horrors of her journey, she maintains the continuity of her descriptions and, by doing so, the continuity of her own sense of identity. As at the outset of her journal when she reminded herself of her place within the landscape, she preserves her connection as she travels. Despite the physical distance between her old and new places, Scott reinforces the continuity of her identity by her repeated use of her Romantic imagery, locating familiar meanings in the new and alien territories she encounters. By doing so, she is able to recognize herself in these places, no matter where she actually is.

Traveling from England to Utah, Mormon journalist Jean Rio Baker faces similar feelings of dislocation with the dramatic alterations in her surroundings. By applying her eloquent and potent descriptions to give meaning to the oceanic and geographic places she encounters on her journey, Baker clarifies the personal significance of these places, making them recognizable through her own interpretations and, by doing so, locating herself in an environment which reflects her own sensibilities and does not challenge her sense of her own identity. Thus, she reinforces her own sense of who she is by making the alien spaces familiar. Fortified by profound religious faith, Baker describes the environments she sees and continually refers to her own spiritual interpretations, as she defines the spaces in the context of the larger religious purpose of her journey. Baker's party included herself and her children: her seventeen-year-old son Walter and his twenty-one-year-old wife, Eliza Ann; William, 15; Edwin, 11; Elizabeth Ann, 9; John, 7; Charles, 6; and Josiah, 4. Baker's journal begins January 4, 1851, and, though her journey ends September 29, she writes several additional entries in October, one in November, one at Christmas, and a final entry on March 22, 1852. Baker's journey begins in Liverpool, England, and she records the three-month voyage to New Orleans. After a brief stay in New Orleans, Baker travels up the Mississippi — rather than the more commonly traveled Missouri River, which was particularly difficult during the spring of 1851 — to St. Louis, where she stayed for one month, then on to Eastern Iowa. By April 22, she and her family had begun the overland portion of their journey. The next seventy-one days were spent crossing 270 miles of Iowa. By July 2, they had arrived at Kanesville (Council Bluffs), where the trip up the Missouri would have taken them. By July 5, they had crossed the Missouri and begun the trip to Salt Lake City, which took eighty-six days (Baker 203–7). She eventually settled in Ogden, Utah, in 1852. Baker later appended her journal on September 29, 1869, and revealed her disappointment with her pilgrimage:

> I have been 18 years in this day, an inhabitant of Utah Territory, and I may say 18 years of hard toil, and almost continual disappointment. . . . I came here in obedience to what I believed to be a revelation of the most High God; trusting the assurance of the Missionaries, whom I believe to have been the spirit of truth, I left my home, sacrificed my property, broke up every dear association, and what was, and is yet, dearer than all, left my beloved native land, and for what? *A Bubble that has burst in my grasp.* (Baker 207)

In November of 1869, Baker moved to California, where she died in 1883 (207).[8]

In her diary of her travels, directed to her relatives and friends in England, she details her sea voyage and overland travel, observing both the land and people she encounters. Continually reminding herself of her journey's purpose as she describes the landscapes before her, Baker copes with her separation from friends and family and reinforces her sense of her identity by maintaining her connection to herself, as well as her family, in her writing. In her opening entry, dated January 4, 1851, the environmental transition she begins figures prominently as she writes: "I this day took leave of every Acquaintance I could collect together, in all probability, never to see them again on earth; I am now (with my children) about to leave ever my Native land, in order to gather with the Church of Christ, in the Valley of the Great Salt Lake, in North America" (212). The separation from her "Native land" is balanced with the knowledge that her destination holds great spiritual significance. As Andrew Hassam has suggested of Australian travel diaries, Baker employs the image of the spiritual journey to the "celestial city" from Bunyan's *Pilgrim's Progress* (45). During her own journey, Baker "mythologizes the landscape" with her personal spiritual meanings and thinks of the "higher destiny" of her migration (45). As Baker departs from her "Native land," a place of personal significance which includes "every Acquaintance" whom she may never see "again on earth, " she adapts to the drastic location changes. By employing her own interpretive frameworks in her descriptions, she reinforces the religious significance, the higher purpose, of her destination as well as the personal meaning of places through which she travels and the people she encounters before reaching Salt Lake City.

Even with the poignancy of her first entry, Baker voices her ease during this expedition to her new home, and her descriptions of the sea reflect her own confidence. On January 25, after "a dreadful night" in the Irish Sea when "the ship has seemed as if she really must turn over," Baker writes, reinforcing her calm, "to myself the sea has never had any terrors, at any time" (213). Even with the dangers of her voyage, she is able to write of her own connection to this particular environment. Like Scott's interconnective description of her home landscape and the new territory she encounters, Baker writes of her own comforting familiarity with the sea. Her description places her within a landscape that, while frightening to others, reinforces her own intimacy with this place. She is not threatened by the sea and never has been. Even though it seems dangerous, because she recognizes this place she does not fear it. She elaborately describes the splendor of the scenery which surrounds her and places herself comfortably within its beauty: "the Moon nearly at full with a deep blue Sky, studded with stars the reflection of which makes the sea appear like an immense sheet of diamonds, and here are we walking the deck at 9 o'clock" (215). She is well rewarded by the beauty that surrounds her. With this description, she locates herself very specifically in the beautiful environment of open ocean. Despite the sea's ability to threaten herself and others bodily, she remains assured and comforted by her knowledge of the sea and her appreciation of its beauty. Clearly she admires both the calm and the power of the sea and, with her admiration, can fearlessly face this powerful but familiar space. Baker continues: "I have seen the mighty deep in its anger with our ship nearly on her beam-ends, and I have seen it, (as now) under a cloudless sky, and scarcely a ripple on its surface, and I do not know which to admire most" (215). For her, the power and beauty of the sea are direct evidence of the divine and thus reinforce her own spiritual understanding of the world and her sense of her own spiritual identity. She closes her entry, "I feel most powerfully the force of those words, 'the Mighty God' which Handel has so beautifully expressed in one of his Chronicles" (215). Baker's descriptions of both the sea's threatening and calm moments reflect and reinforce her belief in "the Mighty God." She seems particularly aware of God's might during the more violent moments even though she assures herself that she is not afraid. Writing these descriptions enables Baker to preserve her own religious sensibilities by exemplifying her reverence of the sea's creator. Though this place is powerful and possibly very dangerous, Baker's personal faith enables her to comprehend the power of the sea not as a threat to her, but rather as evidence of the "Mighty God." As Scott found communion with God and nature in her painstaking descriptions, Baker reinforces her own relationship to this place with the elaborate imagery that constantly reminds her of the security of her faith. For Baker, the power she witnesses in the sea storms is not just evidence of her own small presence before her "Mighty God," but is direct evidence of God. Her faith is not challenged by this dangerous environment but reinforced, and the religious significance of her pilgrimage is reified.

Baker employs her powerful descriptive interpretations as she confronts the death (from unknown causes) of her youngest child, Josiah. Coping with this loss, Baker describes his burial at sea and makes this unmarkable place potent with personal significance. Though she writes, on February 22, of her anguish at his death — "I do feel this trial to be a severe one. I had hoped to have been allowed to take my family safely through the city, *in the tops* of the mountains" (216; original emphasis) — she finds comfort in the sea burial of "the mortal part of my dear Child" (217). Though she cannot describe at length the environment by its distinguishing and symbolic features, she still records the sight of his grave on the open ocean with extreme precision: "44´/14 West. Lat. 25´/13 North." Just as Scott would be able to recognize the places where her mother and brother were buried if she returned there, so too could Baker pinpoint her son's burial place in the open ocean. She also manages to write that the sea remains a soothing presence to her: "I would much rather leave his body in the Ocean than bury him in a strange land, and leave him there" (217). Even with Scott's exacting descriptions, those places could and did become unrecognizable. For Baker, these precise and unchanging numbers will mark her son's grave clearly forever. Baker finds the spiritual consolation from the sea that Scott finds in detailing the locations of her mother's and brother's graves. Dealing with her loss, she continues to write of the sea's beauty and its comfort to her: "Our ship [is] the center of an immense circle, bounded only by the clouds, all is grand and beautiful, and fully repays me for the inconveniences of a Sea Voyage" (218). Placing herself firmly within this environment, she reiterates her small presence in the larger landscape. Despite the severe trial of her child's death and burial at sea, Baker links herself to the environment. Her reward for the "inconveniences" of her voyage is the spectacular representation of God's beauty and power. Even contrasting the peaceful sea with its violence, she remains connected to it: "it was awful, yet grand to look upon the sea, I could only compare it to the boiling of an immense Cauldron, covered with white foam, while the roaring of the winds and waves, was like the bellowing of a thousand wild Bulls . . . I could only look and wonder and admire, for through all our literal ups and downs, I have felt no fear" (220). Baker finds beauty and spiritual restoration in the voyage. Her description shows her special relationship to the sea that explains her understanding of all aspects of the environment. The violence of the sea does not sway her spiritual commitment just as the loss of her son does not. Instead, her descriptions magnify her relationship to the sea and her familiarity with this frightening place. Writing of the beauty of the seascape, she continues to place herself and her personal meanings within the familiar boundaries of her descriptive techniques. She is able to look at the fierce storm and "wonder and admire" the power it represents, a power which she worships but does not fear.

Encountering the new world of America, Baker approaches her descriptions slightly differently. As an English traveler to the United States, Baker adopts sociological observations as a strategy for maintaining her sense of her English identity. Describing the differences between English and American society, she reinforces her own identity through her interpretations of American behavior. As Maria Frawley has suggested of other Victorian travelers, "America was less a place to be enchanted with than a place to scrutinize and assess" (163). When Baker arrives in New Orleans on March 20, her admiration of the landscape continues; however, this new landscape is blighted by slavery. While Baker admires the Mississippi Delta, she writes: "the only thing which deteriorates from its beauty is the sight of hundreds of Negroes at work in the sun. Oh, slavery how I hate thee" (223). Maria Frawley notes that in Harriet Martineau's interpretations of American slavery, she "collapses the boundaries between objective data gatherer and humanitarian emissary" (180). Similarly, Baker distances herself with the analytical details of her descriptions and clearly establishes her difference from the people who participate in the abhorrent slave system. Just as Scott found the slaveholding people of Missouri alienating, Baker also describes New Orleans and slavery as personally repugnant. As she describes the people she encounters, Baker further articulates the significant differences between herself and these others.

Writing of the Americans she meets, Baker humorously ridicules them as she explains, "there is no nobility in America, though never was there a people, fonder of titles, Colonels, Majors, Captains, Judges, and squires, being as plentiful as blackberries" (226). While this description is humorous, Baker details her disturbed response to the lavish slave-holding society she encounters in New Orleans. Meticulously describing the ladies of what she describes as the "Upper-Ten," the highest class in New Orleans social order, Baker writes that these women "dress their slaves even more expensively" than they do themselves in "frocks of embroidered silk, satin, and elegantly worked, muslin trowsers . . . Moroccon walking shoes and white silk stockings" (226). The slaves' elegant attire seems pointlessly extravagant and does not disguise their subordinate position in society. As Baker continues to explain, the elegantly attired slaves' "only business in the streets seems to be to follow the ladies who *own them,* and carry their reticule" (226; original emphasis). Baker seems as repulsed by the extravagance as she does by the slavery. Astonished by their vulgar display, Baker differentiates her own identity through her description. Her most dramatic, powerful confrontation with the condition of slavery also challenges her English sensibilities. Baker continues to express her abhorrence for the slave system. Despite her host Mrs. Blime's opinion "that many of the slaves [in New Orleans] have ten times the comfort of the labourers" in England, Baker writes that during her visit to the female slave market, she could not "help thinking that my friends feelings had become somewhat blunted, if not hardened, by long residence in a slave state" (227). Her own personal beliefs are not swayed by her companion's idealization of the slave system, and she closes her description "in spite of all, the system is a horrid one, to English minds. Well might Sterne say, 'Oh Slavery, disguise thyself as thou wilt, thou are a bitter drought'" (227). Her interpretation of this human landscape is very different from the beauty she detailed on her sea voyage. As she faces the changes the system has inflicted on other visitors, she reconfirms her own English views on slavery. Despite the comfort of the life she sees in New Orleans, she focuses on the "horrible" slave system on which such luxury rests. Strengthened by her "English mind," Baker refuses to be beguiled even though her companion has been "hardened" to its horror. Through her details, she reinforces her sense of herself as English and anti-slavery, and reiterates the strength of her convictions by contrasting her beliefs sharply with those of her friends who have been changed by long residence in this opulent city. Just as Scott contrasted her own sensibilities to the places which lacked her sense of "civilization," Baker relates similarly to the environment of New Orleans. This city has no place for her within it and she clarifies her own differences from its residents in her descriptions. By opposing her own ideas so firmly against the new cultural standards represented in New Orleans, Baker solidifies her distinct sense of who she is, who she is not, and who she will never be.

On May 21, after traveling up the Mississippi to Alexandria, Missouri, Baker closes the section of her journal kept during her sea voyage. She prepares for the changes that will accompany the overland portion of her travels. Returning to the sustaining beauty of the geographic landscape, Baker writes that her journey's "splendid scenery, both wild and beautiful" is something she "never expected to look upon"

(238). Just as Jenny Scott found the landscape rewarding after Missouri, Baker remarks that the scenery "has seemed to repay us for all our inconveniences" (238). She writes to make the transition from the comforting sea voyage to the quite different overland journey. Preparing for the uncomfortable possibilities in this portion of her trip, she writes, "I do not anticipate as much pleasure in our overland journey, as we must expect a life of toil, fatigue, and many privations, to which we are unaccustomed" (238). To deal with these potential difficulties, as well as her possible fear of more problems, she writes of the natural places through which she has already traveled, as if to fortify her sense of purpose for the coming challenge:

> when I recall to mind the various scenes through which we have passed, and the thousands of miles we have travelled, during the last three weeks or I would say the last three months, and the manifold instances of preserving mercy we have received at the hands of our Heavenly Father, I doubt not I shall still, (If I remain faithful) enjoy the same protection, upon the land, as I have done upon the waters. (238)

Preparing her journal to send to her friends and family in England, Baker explains that she understands the hardships she faces and that she will be prepared for any events that may occur. While she recognizes the possible loss of her faith and the subsequent change in her spiritual understanding, she reinforces her journey's divine purpose by remembering the "manifold instances of preserving mercy" she has received "at the hands of our Heavenly Father." As she reinforces her religious beliefs with the evidence she has seen in the last three months of her journey, she begins to prepare for the next challenges she may face on her overland trip. And while she admits the possibility of dramatic change to her own identity — she may lose her faith — she reassures herself that if she remains "faithful" she will certainly "enjoy the same protection" as she has previously. This is a powerful incentive to maintain her own sense of identity throughout the rest of her travels. Thus, to ensure such continuity, Baker invokes comforting imagery with which she is most familiar and by which she is most powerfully reassured. If she remains her faithful self, she will continue to be protected by that faith.

Even though the overland journey is more difficult than the sea voyage, Baker employs her descriptions similarly, elaborating on the familiar imagery she sees in her sur- roundings. Just as she admired the beauty of the open ocean under the stars, she describes the prairie's encircling envi- ronment and focuses on the immense space surrounding her. Just as she was comforted by her sea descriptions, she reiterates the sense of peacefulness and security that she feels in such a wondrous place:

> I thought of you all, and what you would say, could you see us, sitting in the open air, with nothing to tell us of the living world, but the croaking of the frogs, in the spring time near us, the stars glitter- ing in the heavens, and the moon shining brightly, enabling us to see for miles around us, I felt at the moment a sense of security and freedom, I cannot describe, and retired to rest, with a thankful heart, that we are brought thus far, in safety. (242–43)

Writing of this place, Baker affirms her own "sense of security and freedom" and her faith. While she admitted previously to the potential loss of her faith, she remains humble and "thankful" that she has been kept in safety. By continuing to recognize the familiar beauty in these new territories, she remains faithful to her beliefs and to her own sense of herself. In the beauty and majesty of the open prairie, Baker recognizes her own place in this new and comfortable space. Just as Alexandra Bergson in Willa Cather's *O Pioneers!* watches the "ordered march" of stars and, in the "great operations of nature" and "the law that lay behind them," feels a "sense of personal security" (40), Baker discovers "security and freedom" in the landscape she sees.

As she encounters more people on her Overland journey, Baker again adopts the sociological voice of a Victorian traveler as a means of distinguishing herself from the people she meets. If she studies people with this kind of scientific distance, she can maintain her sense of herself as distinct from the Americans. Even when she does admire certain qualities they possess, these qualities are her own and reflect her own sensibilities. While her descriptions of the New Orleans society reinforced her ideological differences, her descriptions of more "common" Americans seems to identify the success of the democratic experiment in the United States and to link these values with her own English ones. Maria Frawley suggests English Victorian women travelers were particularly interested in the differences that made America "more like home and less like home than any other part of the world" (162). In examining the differences between Europe and the United States, travelers "scoured the country to discover the effects and implications" of the more traditional "forms of authority" which did not operate in the new country (162). As Baker crosses the countryside, she elaborates on the advantages she sees in the American democracy. Clearly she prefers the independent self-sufficient farmer to the

immoderate and seemingly decadent residents of New
Orleans. Unlike her descriptions of the port city — in which
she sought to differentiate herself from the moral decline
apparent in the city — in these descriptions Baker represents
the "American farmer" with positive attributes with which
she can identify. She is willing to assimilate these qualities
into her self-perception because they are already so familiar
and acceptable to her that she need not alter her own sense of
self. Baker does not assimilate these qualities so much as she
sees these qualities as reflective of her own familiar values.
Thus she sees herself in these farmers and knows these people
just as she knows her own self. The people here do not lead
the same alien and decadent lifestyle as those she encountered
in New Orleans. She writes, "nothing can exceed the kindness
of the people as we pass along, many a time, when our wagons
have been in a mudhole that men working in the fields have,
have left their ploughs to come and help us. . . . it seems a rule
among them to help every one who is in need" (245). As
Baker encounters helpful people, she elaborates on her interpretation of their situation:

> I often think that there is no person so thoroughly
> independent as the American farmer, his land is his
> own, beef, mutton, pork, and poultry, shears his
> own sheep, and his wife spins the wool, dyes it of
> various colours, and in many cases weaves it into
> cloth for dresses, and other articles of clothing,
> Blankets, flannels. I have been in many a farm-
> house, and never could discover, any thing like
> scarcity of comforts of life, their furniture is plain,
> but good of its kind, and in most cases, their houses
> are very clean. (246)

In contrast to the decadence of New Orleans and its slave system, here Baker describes the modesty and self-sufficiency of the American farmer. As she does so, she praises the positive democratic structure of her new homeland, which allows, and even encourages, the self-reliance and independence of its citizens, qualities she herself admires and recognizes as her own. As she begins to identify her own sensibilities and values in these places, she focuses on the freedoms which enable Americans to exist without the authority inherent in European systems. While she had previously affirmed the strength of her "English mind" to resist slavery, she now confirms the promising attributes of the American life. While her sociological descriptions then affirmed her identity as an English traveler, they now serve to acclimate her to the new environment by identifying the qualities she finds most attractive and acceptable in the American frontier as similar to her own.

As Baker details the new environment, she also reinforces the similarities between this new country and her previous home. Describing the prairie, she writes of the "great variety of flowers growing on the prairie, such as are cultivated in our gardens at home" (248). Listing the flowers she recognizes and describing their natural appearance on the prairie, Baker identifies the prairie as familiar, just as Scott did during her own horticultural descriptions. The flowers — "violets, primroses, daisy's, bluebells, the lily of the valley, columbines, of every shade, from white to deepest purple, Virginia stocks in large patches, the wild rose too is very plentiful, perfuming the air, for miles" (248) — are combined "with a numerous variety of beautiful plants, whose names are unknown" (248) to her. Here she co-mingles the new scenery with familiar and recognizable imagery of her English homeland and the details of her own cultivated garden. As with her descriptions of the independent American farmer, this independent and uncultivated garden reflects the natural freedoms available within the United States, but it is not so unrecognizable that Baker is alienated from her new residence.

This landscape is not always so serene, and Baker continues to balance the frightening aspects of her new environment with her marvelous descriptions of its beauty. Just as in her descriptions of the stormy sea voyage, Baker's description of prairie storms reveals her understanding of the power of the natural environment: "while I am now writing the claps of thunder are awful, they seem to be all round us at once, our vehicles shake violently at every clap." Even while this experience seems alarming, Baker explains, "we are quite snug in our castles" (249). Even in the midst of danger she remains safe and is ultimately rewarded because of her self-assurance. Closing her entry, she recaptures the serenity after the torrent. Just as she balanced her descriptions of the powerful sea storms with imagery of the calm ocean, here she compensates for this storm's violence with rewarding and peaceful description: "after the rain cleared we saw myriads of fire-flies the first we had ever seen, and I thought them the most beautiful natural phenomena, I had ever beheld" (249).

By September 26, as Baker moves closer to her final destination, she expresses her mounting admiration for this new land and seems to prove its divinity. The landscape is now "beyond description for wilderness and beauty," and Baker writes that she is "indeed among the everlasting Hills" (274). Her appreciative description of the landscape reiterates her belief in the majesty of God's creation. "The splendid scenery" is countered by "awful roads," but she describes her surroundings with wonder, showing that even though the travel is difficult and strenuous, she is rewarded by the amazing scenery:

> the mountains on each side of us seem to be solid rock, but in crevices on their sides trees are growing in abundance, and the tops covered with groves of splendid fir-trees; in some places large pieces of rock have been detached, and have rolled down the mountain side, many of them as large as a small house, in some instances, the rocks lie directly across the road, which occasion much difficulty in travelling, in one spot, the rocks had the appearance of a ruinous gateway. (274)

Despite the difficulty of traveling as well as the apparent danger of this journey, Baker writes that "the grandeur of the scenery to my mind takes away all fear" (274), a description reminiscent of her tumultuous ocean scenes. This dramatic landscape triggers her "admiration" and her spiritual description. Just as she thought of Handel's praise of "God's majesty," she writes, "Milton's expressions in Paradise Lost came forcibly to my recollections — 'These are thy glorious works, Parent of good, in wisdom thou hast made them all'"(275).[9] Writing of this power, she is able "to forget all the hardships" of her journey and confirm her reasons for her journey. In addition to the "grandeur" she writes of here, she continues to find affirmation of her religious identity as she continues to describe the landscape. As Anne Farrar Hyde has suggested of American landscape aesthetics, these powerful places represent the "revered expression of God's will" (18). Unlike European landscapes, the American landscape, "the true wilderness[,] . . . could show the intentions and power of God" (18). Described as "sublime," the American landscape thus gained significance over the culture offered by Europe (19). Detailing her surroundings, Baker applies her own interpretive frameworks, which reflect her cultural consciousness and have served to reinforce her own sense of her identity throughout her journey. For Baker, the journey she describes as "long and perilous" (277) is also one of divine beauty. In the landscapes surrounding her, she sees her own faith magnified in the grandeur and power of the natural settings and she is assured of this new territory's familiarity and significance. Rather than allowing the physical dislocation to displace her own sense of herself, Baker locates herself in this place by reiterating her own ideology and recognizing the similarities between her current surroundings and her previous home. Writing of awe-inspiring images which indicate the presence of her "Mighty God," Baker is able to recognize and make familiar these strange spaces. As Jenny Scott viewed the landscape as a beautiful comfort against the horror of her journey, Jean Rio Baker describes the scenery for similar comfort as well as justification for her own migration.

Both Scott and Baker apply personal and cultural interpretations which served them in their previous places. These interpretations make the new territory comprehensible and therefore much less threatening to their sense of who they are. As Paul Carter has argued, the travel journal is "an act of language" that brings "living space into being and render[s] it habitable" (144). Within the personal texts kept by travelers and explorers to Australia, Carter suggests, it is possible "to discern the process of transforming space into place" (xxiii). Rather than alter their own sense of their identity as they confront these dramatically different and unknown territories, Scott and Baker re-form these new sites to meet their expectations. By making these spaces recognizable, by making them significant *places*, both women are able to manipulate what is outside their control — their environment — through what is within their control — their interpretations of that environment — and which generates from their sense of their own identity.

According to Andrew Hassam, one of the motives for keeping a travel diary arises from "the novelty of being transported to an alien environment" (37). Maintaining a travel diary, he suggests, "entails the projection of the diarist as protagonist into an alien geographical environment" (37). Similarly, Gayle Davis suggests that one such motivating factor for the Victorian woman on the American frontier was the maintenance of her self-image as a Victorian lady, for "the more her identity was threatened, the more crucial writing became" (8). Thus the new geographical environment was controlled through narration and description. In the case of these two diarists, controlling their own interpretations also allowed Scott and Baker to recognize these new environments and to make them familiar. This recognition enabled both women to adapt their surroundings to themselves as much or more than they had to adapt themselves to the new country. Rather than control the actual places, these women control their interpretations of these new places and maintain their own identities as they locate themselves and their sensibilities in their landscapes. As each constructs her relationship to her surroundings, each applies a personal meaning to the locations in which she finds herself. Scott signifies her places with the romantic imagery she finds comforting. Baker reiterates her spiritual purpose by imbuing the environment with divine significance. Dorothy Jones suggests that such landscape description and mapping "results from attempts to accommodate the alien and unfamiliar within the myths and images derived from European culture" (64). For women crossing the Overland Trail, placing the landscapes in the context of their own personal and cultural mythologies enabled them to maintain the continuity of their identities. Rather than alter their own sense of who they were out of the places they had been, as they traveled through alien environments, these women interpreted the new places with familiar and comforting imagery, which made these frighteningly strange places manageable. These very different environments could be governed as long as the women were able to apply their own interpretive frameworks to the new places and people they encountered. Gloria Anzaldúa explains that she writes "because the world I create in the writing compensates for what the real world does not give me. By writing I put order in the world, give it a handle so I can grasp it" (169). By manipulating the places in their writing and descriptions, Scott and Baker create the environments they need to relieve their sense of dislocation. Rather than remain misplaced, they place themselves with these descriptions, recognizing their own sensibilities in their surroundings. In writing, these women carry their landscapes with them. While they are clearly out of place, their interpretive frameworks make the landscapes recognizable consistently. Using their own religious, intellectual, and philosophical frameworks, Scott and Baker are able to place themselves within these new areas no matter how alien the environment actually is. In facing any threats encountered on the journey, they are able to maintain their identities by writing through these challenges. For these women, their temporary position within a threatening but linguistically manageable environment lasted only a few months. Their journals, ended at the close of their travel, do not show any changes these women may have undergone as they were challenged by life on the frontier. The finite nature of the journey and these diaries offers only a brief vision of how women managed their sense of themselves as they traveled to the frontier in Western United States.

TWO

Narratives of Resistance
Negotiating Abuse and the Endangered Self

Then the shadows had begun to gather; it was as if Osmond deliberately, almost malignantly put the lights out one by one. The dusk at first was vague and thin, and she could still see her way in it. But it steadily deepened, and if now and again it occasionally lifted there were certain corners that were impenetrably black. These shadows were not an emanation from her own mind; she was sure of that; she had done her best to be just and temperate, to see only the truth. They were a part, they were a kind of creation and consequence of her husband's very presence.

HENRY JAMES, *THE PORTRAIT OF A LADY*

enry James's enigmatic novel *The Portrait of a Lady* follows Isabel Archer's slow and painful transformation as she struggles to maintain her own sense of her identity against the competing identities imposed on her by her family, friends, and most insidiously, her husband. Their narratives, fueled by cultural ideology and personal enmity, encompass Isabel's own, influencing her self-understanding as she attempts to remain "true" to her own sense of who she is. James's fiction is emblematic of the lives of two nineteenth-century women whose diaries illuminate their similar struggles with self-understanding and self-representation. Written during the mid-nineteenth through late-nineteenth century, the diaries of Henrietta Baker Embree and Tennessee Keys Embree exemplify the complicated and sometimes disturbing process of self-understanding, and disclose the powerful personal influences that affect these women's sense of themselves. Illustrating their writers' adaptations during their sequential marriages to Dr. John Wilhoit Embree,[1] the diaries reveal that both marriages were at least psychologically, and possibly physically, abusive; each woman exhibits behavior more commonly known today as "battered woman syndrome."[2] More interestingly, these diaries articulate the subtle techniques each woman used to resist the psychological abuse of Dr. Embree and to reinforce, adapt, or redefine herself during her life. As Henrietta and Tennessee describe their lives and the lives of their children in their diaries, they use their autobiographical writing concurrently to maintain their own sense of their identity, to adapt their sense of who they are, and to contest the identity imposed by their husband. Though Dr. Embree's influence has an eventual, detrimental impact on both women, their diaries serve to counteract the effects of his continued psychological and physical abuse by allowing each woman to challenge Embree's imposed identities. Reconstructing their own identities for themselves, their children, and families, Henrietta and Tennessee contradict his definitions, defy his interpretation by detailing their own self-understanding, and, through their writing, "exchange the position of object for the subjectivity of self-representational agency" (Gilmore 12). As Henrietta and Tennessee tell their own stories to themselves as well as to their children, each uses her diary "as a discourse of re-membering and self-restoration" (Gilmore 90). Their journals reveal how external forces alter their self-definitions, and how each woman negotiates these alterations as she writes her own "narrative of resistance" through which she can "experience both self-discovery and self-recovery" (hooks 72).

In *The Tapestries of Life*, Bettina Aptheker argues, "what constitutes resistance is framed within the context of women's practical, material, personal and psychological resources" (218). Aptheker suggests the oral histories of battered women "show us that women's resistance is along a continuum in which the personal and political are inextricably woven" (218). Similarly, Estelle Jelinek suggests that women's "autobiographical intention is often powered by the motive to convince readers of their self-worth, to clarify, to affirm, and to authenticate their feelings" (*Women's Autobiography* 15). In *Autobiographics: A Feminist Theory of Women's Self-Representation* (1994), Leigh Gilmore suggests autobiography itself is a "site of resistance, " because it "engages the politics of looking back and challenges the politics of how the past and present may be known in a particular version of history" (80). While Gilmore does not use diaries in her discussion, these autobiographical writings also reveal similar strategies of self-representation. Focusing on "women's autobiographical production" (x), Gilmore formulates a theoretical approach which examines *autobiographics,* "the interruptions and eruptions . . . resistance and contradiction [which serve as] strategies of self-representation" (42). Because "the practice of writing an autobiography" gives the writer access to self-definition, Gilmore suggests, access to autobiography "means access to the identity it constructs" (xv). Thus, the "autobiographical subject is produced not by experience but by autobiography" (25). In other words, interpreting experience through autobiography, by *representing* this experience and a version (or several versions) of a 'self' in autobiographical writing, is what makes that experience comprehensible, and makes that represented 'self' possible. In the case of the diaries I will consider here, as each woman can become more like the person she writes herself as in her diary, she reinforces her resistance and her interpretations by writing down the evidence to be read by herself and someone else. As Gilmore argues, by "representing herself in opposition to a certain standard of 'truth,'" she becomes an agent in her own narrative, "seizing upon self-representation as a strategy to change one's life story" (33). Through their diaries, these women resist Dr. Embree's standard of truth, attempting to gain control of their own identity, and access the identity created within their autobiographical writing. Unfortunately, despite this opposition, their writing also reveals how Embree's continued criticism influences and alters both women's self-concepts. However, as Gilmore continues, "autobiographical identity and agency are not identical to identity and agency in 'real life'; rather they are its representation, and that representation . . . is its construction" (48).

Thus, though what Henrietta and Tennessee write, and what we can perceive as their attempts to gain agency through writing, may have enabled them to exist and to resist Embree's abuse psychologically, the representation or construction of agency may not have survived beyond the writing of it. In *The Auto/Biographical I* (1992), Liz Stanley argues that feminist "auto/biography" should recognize the "complex views of the self" rather than "eradicate" them in the search for "a seamless truth" (11). Rather, Stanley suggests, autobiographical selves are "both whole or struggling to be become so *and* deeply and irresolvably fractured" (14; emphasis added). Each of the Embree diaries requires readers to recognize that these writers were, as Stanley phrases it, "like this *and* like that" (163). Though each woman wrote with her own individual style, both journals are painful records of inward turmoil and spiritual decline as each woman tries to survive in her isolating and abusive marriage. Defining themselves against or with Embree's image of who they are, both Henrietta and Tennessee find it increasingly difficult to achieve an autonomous identity. Thus, as they represent themselves to their children and to themselves, Henrietta and Tennessee alter their self-perceptions and self-understandings, stabilizing their identities throughout a lifetime of adaptations.

It is important to note that both of these diaries are available only in typescripts. According to the typescript, after Henrietta's death and prior to transcription, her manuscript diary was first in the possession of Margaret Graves, Henrietta's sister-in-law, and then Tennessee Embree's daughter Gillian Embree Creswell, the original inheritor of Tennessee's journal. Henrietta Embree's typescript is dated 1928. Tennessee Embree's typescript is dated 1941. While both typescripts indicate that the originals of each diary were in the possession of Creswell when the typescripts were donated to the University of Texas, the manuscripts have not been located, so a comparison which might indicate textual alterations cannot be made at this time.[3]

The typescript of Henrietta Embree's diary begins January 1, 1856 (when Henrietta is nearly twenty-two), and concludes with an undated entry which seems close to her death, at twenty-nine, from tuberculosis in June of 1863. Her journal is intended to serve as a long intimate conversation with her sister Jennie in Kentucky and as a written legacy for her daughter. The first year of her diary (1856) details her friendships, her anguish over the death of her infant daughter Mollie, and her bouts of depression. Since she suffers from consumption, much of her writing is concerned with her eventual death, and her desire to be remembered is evident throughout her diary. As Henrietta explains, her writing must speak for her if she is unable to do so herself. Using her writing to maintain her relationship to her family, her daughter Nattie, and her friends, she addresses her "dear old blue book" and writes, "you will not let my loved friends forget me" (69a). While she feels she cannot "confide any deep imotion" (75), she uses her journal to speak for her, hoping it will "reveal to them that, that never would have been known had you not of spoke it" (69a). Her intention to leave a written record of her private thoughts is clear early in her writing and, as Gilmore has suggested, her diary provides Henrietta access to autobiographical self-representation which may counter other images of her.

Serving a similar purpose, Tennessee's journal[4] of her married life (1865–84), in the growing community of Belton, Texas, is written specifically for her infant daughter Beulah, who is named for the independent main character in Augusta Evans Wilson's 1859 novel, *Beulah*. She explains in her opening entry, "the thought occurred to me that it would greatly interest my little 'Beulah' in after years to read her mother's journal kept while she was a child" (September 25, 1865). Additionally, Tennessee addresses her eleven-year-old stepdaughter Nattie, with whom she strives to build a relationship. As Harriet Blodgett notes of this common practice, by reading their mothers' journals, "children will learn what their mothers were like as individuals and, mothers may hope, come to understand and admire or, if necessary, forgive" (73). In this case, Tennessee explains her own sense of herself as she resists the defining influence of her husband. The journal becomes a more important companion for herself, however, as she strives to find the emotional intimacy she lacks in her marriage and struggles to comprehend her husband's psychologically abusive behavior, which includes angry tirades, derogatory comments, drunken binges, and physical assaults on Beulah. As well as her intention to write for her child, Tennessee writes to find companionship, explaining "my heart still pouts for a lady confidant" (September 28, 1865). Unlike Henrietta, who maintained friendships with several women, Tennessee seems more isolated than her predecessor. Writing to her infant daughter alleviates her isolation as she struggles to present herself and reinforce her own sense of her identity.

In both Henrietta and Tennessee's diaries, the audience plays a pivotal role for the writers. Both writers are aware of their audience outside their diary pages and each firmly intends, or at least hopes, that the diary will serve to allow others, primarily both women's daughters, to understand their lives. Lynn Z. Bloom suggests in her study "I Write for Myself and Strangers: Private Diaries as Public Documents," diaries like the Embrees' are not "truly private" but rather "public documents" which employ certain stylistic devices "to develop and contextualize the subject and thus aid in orienting the work to an external audience" (29). Indeed, Henrietta and Tennessee create their receptive audience specifically as an ally to whom they can communicate and who will support their resistance. By writing to this specific audience, each could reveal their attempts to resist Dr. Embree's influence and his 'truth,' and by constructing such resistance in writing, could achieve "autobiographical identity and agency" (Gilmore 48) even if it was denied them in 'real life.' This "self-representational agency" gained by explaining themselves continually to their chosen audiences serves to validate their lives and empower each writer.

The need for such a sympathetic audience develops as Henrietta's marital difficulties become apparent. After sporadic entries in 1857 and none in 1858, she resumes her diary in January of 1859 and begins to elaborate specifically her struggles with Dr. Embree's critical psychological manipulation, her deepening isolation, and her resulting identity adaptations. She writes that a "veil of sorrow has enveloped" her husband and relates that she "must not look cast down, at least as long as [my] husband is" (74). While she tries to maintain a cheerful attitude for Embree's sake, Henrietta becomes a target for his dark and increasingly violent moods. As she writes, she details her responsibility for his behavior as she explains, "I know my own temper has caused it all — and involved the *one dearest to me of all* other — Yes when I knew that I caused that *one* to sin — Should I not weep bitter tears clothed in sackcloth and ashes" (75). Even though she blames her own temper for her husband's "sin," she also refuses to overemphasize the "sin," writing, "it is done and I can do no more than mourn — over it" (75). Nevertheless, the incident affects her as she tries to alter her own behavior for the future. As much as she attempts to avoid feeling responsible, Henrietta acquiesces as she writes, as if she has talked herself out of any stronger feeling against her husband. While she first attempts to brush off the incident, she does continue to focus on her failure. As she assigns blame to herself for this unexplained crisis in her marriage, her deep emotional anguish over this experience is evident. While she previously denied that what she writes in her journal is truly "deep imotion," she ponders her own misery and writes, "I am wondering if I ever shall be happy more" (75). While Henrietta attempts to use writing as a form of resistance to her own torment, her response to the consequences of her action seem to belie its effectiveness. However, as she turns the blame on herself, she also takes control by rendering her actions as important influences on her husband's behavior.

While Henrietta's acceptance of fault can be read as a pattern of "blaming the victim" (Andreadis 189), these self-directed comments may indeed serve an additional psychological purpose as she tries to establish "perceived control" in her life (Miller and Porter 140). In their study of twentieth-century battered women, "Self Blame in Victims of Violence," Dale T. Miller and Carol A. Porter note that despite traditional views of self-blame, "the degree of self-blame evidenced by victims correlate[s] positively with subsequent coping" (139). While Henrietta's self-denigration is painful to read, it may be the only form of control she can take in her life. As Miller and Porter explain, "acceptance of responsibility enables [victims] to maintain the belief that they are in control of their lives" (140). Using this technique, Henrietta controls her interpretations of events if not the events themselves. Liz Stanley cautions, "'power' and 'powerlessness' are complex matters . . . [and] often co-exist in the same piece of behavior done by the same person at exactly the same moment in time" (165). Even though Henrietta claims responsibility for her husband's moods, she also resists. She expresses contempt for her husband's "blues," writing "how I detest them. I use[d] to have [these spells] but now I have too much disgust for them — to let them find a comfortable seat in my heart" (87). Her defiance here is an interesting counterpoint to her own previous depressive episodes. Now she refuses to allow herself to feel "blue" and implies a certain weakness in her husband's acceptance of his moods. By expressing her contempt in her journal, she can shore up her strength and display her ability to survive these difficult circumstances.

After a lengthy illness during April of 1859, Henrietta resumes her journal, and further explores the dynamics between herself and her husband. Specifying a particular incident that illuminates a seemingly familiar pattern in their marriage, Henrietta writes: "the Dr and I ate alone, consequently we got into a warm argument — the subject being, the inconstancy of women — my already wounded spirits were not at all healed — but chafed over again" (108). While she clearly is able to disagree with her husband, she is at a disadvantage with her "already wounded spirits" and the doctor's private psychological assault on his wife and her "inconstancy" clearly serves to undermine her self-confidence and self-understanding. As he subtly and overtly weakens Henrietta's defenses, she must choose alternative ways to resist his protracted critiques, even as she tries to comprehend his alienating behavior.[5]

As Henrietta's despair intensifies, she details more specifically her difficulties in making her family happy and writes of her desperate desire to find guidance as she struggles to cope with her husband's behavior. While she writes that "one could not . . . labor harder" to try and make her family happy, she cannot seem to succeed: "I fall short in the attempt — and am blamed" (122). She attempts to counter outside criticisms by relating her labors and the blame which falls on her. She hopes for "some one to go before and tell me of my duty" because "to be dependent on ones self, to know, and do what is right" seems particularly difficult (122). She also blames herself for her inability to cope with her emotions, "with the temper to contend with that I have — and then many unmentionable trials, that the world knoweth not off" (122). While she had previously argued with Dr. Embree, Henrietta now despairs and reveals her anxiety as she expresses her declining self-regard, her difficulty in comprehending where her duties lie, and her desire for some emotional support and comfort in carrying out these duties. Her isolation is not only literal but figurative. Even though she has the companionship of her husband, he continually finds fault with her work, her temper, and her gender. She explains that there are "unmentionable trials" that she *must* keep from the world and her sister, difficulties which she recognizes as almost overwhelming. However, Henrietta tries to assuage her own concern, as well as her sister's, by denying any significance to her dark moods as she acknowledges her acceptance of them: "I indulge in tenebrious spells much . . . more than I should, and yet I never expect to get rid of them, but suspect they will grow on me as moss upon a ruted stone" (123). Unlike her previous admission that she had too much "contempt" to allow her "spells" to continue, Henrietta now shifts dramatically, accepting the inevitability of her "blues." While she still admits to "indulging," she now seems complacent, even helpless, about her ability to effect any real change. Her anger dissipating, Henrietta struggles to find a reason for her own unhappiness, despite her seemingly satisfying life. Exposing her torment and denigrating rationalizations, she deliberates, "I feel as if there is no pleasure for me perhaps I do not deserve it" (142).

Trying to identify the cause of her dissatisfaction, Henrietta ponders, "it seems that I have that that should give me happiness children two sweet and as dear to me as my own life — and yet I am not happy" (142). It is not her children who limit her happiness and she writes that she does actually know why she is miserable though she "yet forbear[s], to pencil" the reason within her journal. Despite her apprehension about writing the cause of her depression, she does reveal the reasons, explaining, "I am a strange creature for I cannot live without love — especially without the love of those that I love" (142). Her emotional isolation, and its cause, is clear as she questions, "why should I be dependent why not be indipendent? is there a species of my composition? . . . Jen may you never experience none of those feelings I am now contending with" (142). As she admits that her children love her, she exposes her loveless marriage. Her alienation is graphically portrayed as she asks for a companion, "some species of my composition," to offer her the love she needs. Her husband, she implies, is not even human, or at least seems as foreign to her as some alien creature. Yet her blame is self-directed as she explains that *she* is the "strange creature," rather than her husband. She focuses on her own responsibility for her misery and, unlike in previous entries, makes no effort to deny this self-destructive criticism.

Attempting to comprehend her emotional instability, Henrietta turns to her own family heritage to discover a cause for her unhappiness. By doing so, she discounts any other causes she may have mentioned previously that influence her moods. If her emotional turmoil stems from an hereditary cause, she can avoid feeling quite so responsible for them. She laments the possibility that her own daughter may suffer with the "same horrible spells" that her mother, grandfather, and great-grandfather experienced (142a). Henrietta, while understanding the hereditary nature of her depressive episodes, blames herself for passing on the "wretched heirloom" (142a). Unlike her previous entries where she discussed her actions or behavior as the reason for her own difficulties, she now finds a different cause for her moods. Here Henrietta resorts to blaming her own heredity rather than her actions. As a form of "characterological blame," identifying this family trait as the cause of her crisis may "undermine the perception of control" and "lead to feelings of depression and despair" (Miller and Porter 147). As Henrietta searches for a reason for her tumultuous emotions, she loses the sense of control over her situation. Her downward spiral begins as she relinquishes the convictions which she employed to resist her husband's degradation and to maintain her psychological strength.

Struggling to hide her feelings from her family, Henrietta relies extensively on her sister, expressing in her diary what she cannot in her home and exploring the slow deterioration of her internal support system. While addressing her sister has previously allowed Henrietta a spiritual connection, she now feels more isolated. As this relationship begins to fail her, she temporarily loses her desire to write: "I have almost quit journalizing entirely, I reckoned the cost perhaps and found it would not pay to keep it up" (161). She is no longer even able to find the value she once had in communicating with her sister and she loses another method of, as well as her desire for, self-preservation. She explains her own feelings of worthlessness, showing how her desire for her own self-assurance has withered. She now turns to self-castigation, writing, "May you Jen, never feel as little account as I do" (162). Comparing herself to her aunt whose journal she found "entertaining" and "improving," Henrietta denigrates herself, revealing her deep despair as she can now see only her own failures as she compares herself to her aunt: "Oh that I was only half as good as Jennie — I would then with *sealed lips and smiling countenance* go through the world pleasantly, and without a murmur — but as I get older I grow worse" (173; original emphasis). While her comments are self-denigrating, Henrietta also valorizes her resistance by emphasizing her inability to fake her marital happiness. While she may not be as "good" as her aunt, she cannot allow this falsehood to persist, covering her unhappiness with the "sealed lips and smiling countenance." Nonetheless, her uncertainty and helplessness are equally influential and she explains "this eve finds me floating down the stream whenever the current may take me — not making a feeble effort to save my self. It has been a gloomy day" (174). Her resistance turns to hopelessness, graphically portrayed in her elaborate metaphor, and the recognition that she is not making even a "feeble effort" to save herself.

Her self-destruction seems inevitable as she describes her failing physical health: "one week ago today I had quite a hemorage of my right lung" (175). Recognizing that both her lungs are affected and faced with an imminent death, Henrietta begins to write with added purpose: "I feel that I am but a short sojourner here, then how very necessary it is for me to spend all of my precious moments in getting ready for the great change that soon must come upon me" (175). As much as she disparaged her writing's value, her journal takes on additional significance during these final entries while she tried to communicate and manage her fear as she attempts to write her own experience of the "great change."[6]

Knowing that her diary will outlast her, Henrietta tries to explain her emotions for her readers and again exposes the estranged and difficult marriage. She turns to her journal to deal with her distress and relates her husband's angry and indifferent response to her illness. In describing his angry response, Henrietta displays clearly her need for her writing, now the only companion she can turn to in order to alleviate her spiritual as well as physical suffering. Even though she admits to hiding "even my hearts secrets from" her journal, Henrietta poignantly describes her emotional distress, writing "perhaps it was better if I only spoke to you on all of my subjects at least — You it would not weary nay *make* angry" (176). She writes, "it is to you my old friend I come confiding my most intence wish — so when I am tempted to fill anothers ear — with my complaints I can turn to this page" (176). Apparently her husband does not, or will not, offer any comfort to his dying wife and she must turn to writing to cope with his anger. In addition, Henrietta can prevent her own psychological anguish by writing, rather than speaking. She also denies the emotional impact of his anger, explaining, "it makes no difference" (176). Rather than blame Dr. Embree, Henrietta writes of her own responsibility toward him: "my husband you will never know how

much I love you — there is a want of understanding in
my nature on your part, or at least I think so" (176). Even
though Henrietta accepts blame for Embree's "coldness,"
she tries to adapt quickly to his indifference, writing "let
it all go for what it is worth, only save me my book from
annoying — my dear husband, with tails of my aches pains
and afflicktions — Oh may I be enabled to bear them, here
after philosphicklly — at least let me suffer here after, in
silence" (176). While Henrietta previously resisted through
her writing, she acquiesces to her own silencing, preferring
to write of her fears as she attempts to reinforce her own
strength through this private expression. Though she
qualifies her self-doubt, she blames herself for a "want of
understanding." She also writes her own rejection of his
reproach as she attempts to shrug off the significance of his
actions, writing "let it all go for what it is worth." This pattern is typical of battered women who experience an
"increasing sense of helplessness and hopelessness" which is
"reinforced by a sense of isolation and poor self-esteem, fos-
tered by the batterer." Victims eventually begin "to deny and
minimize" the violence (Jaffe et al. 23). While this may not
seem to be a very powerful rejection of her husband's anger,
Henrietta's continued use of this technique in her writing
reveals that this may be her own best coping device when
dealing with her husband's behavior. In her journal, she can
refuse responsibility that she may have been forced to assume
more publicly.

In her final undated entry, Henrietta seems close to her
death at the age of twenty-nine, two years from her last dated
entry in 1861.[7] She strives to relate her own peace of mind
to her reader as she faces death. She offers the "one good
thing" she has to "communicate" in her "dear book" (176).

Her diary and her faith are all that remain to help her to comprehend her sense of failure in all other areas: "my faith is stronger than ever was before. . . . I feel weak but I hope God will not forsake me but give me strength to do his will" (176). Henrietta has again turned to her writing to keep her voice alive for her readers. She seems particularly willing to die as it means she will be released from her earthly suffering. What she has used to explore and to understand her life — her faith, her communion with her sister, her writing — have nearly disappeared. What little remains of this support system cannot keep her emotionally alive. As her body wastes, so too does her psychological connection with her sister and her ability to communicate through writing. Her physical wasting from tuberculosis and her resulting death, most likely from inanition and the lack of sufficient physical nourishment, darkly mirrors her emotional death from an equally lethal emptiness of spirit.

The misery of Henrietta's experience is compounded by the diary of Dr. Embree's second wife, Tennessee Keys.[8] The twenty-four-year-old Tennessee married the thirty-six-year-old widower on July 21, 1864, one year, one month, and eight days after Henrietta's death.[9] Tennessee's diary of her married life spans nineteen years, 1865 through 1884, and tragically echoes Henrietta's spiritual and physical decline. Tennessee's journal also displays her deterioration more graphically as it offers a glimpse into Tennessee's life prior to her marriage and records the marriage's development after the first year. Tennessee notes that "the Doctor is different in his nature" (September 30, 1865). She, like Henrietta, seems to accept his difference even as she is perplexed by it. Like Henrietta's desire for "a species of my own composition," and her inability to live "without the love of those I

love" (142), Tennessee writes to find a similar companionship because her experience with Embree seems equally
alienating. Despite Henrietta and Tennessee's different writing styles, the similarities between both women's emotional
response to Dr. Embree is striking. Tennessee writes of her
experiences with Dr. Embree's "nature," and her descriptions of her responses resound painfully with Henrietta's
voice, as Embree's second wife frequently repeats questions
similar to those posed by his first. While Tennessee seems
emotionally and physically stronger, perhaps only because she
is not suffering from tuberculosis, the changes she undergoes
and the adaptations she makes often duplicate Henrietta's
previous alterations. Like Henrietta, Tennessee reveals her own
slow spiritual consumption as she struggles to understand her
relationship with her husband and adapt to life with him.

As she explains her behavior to her daughter Beulah,
Tennessee remarks proudly that, even if it is difficult, she
"can almost govern [her temper] now to [her] will" (October 3, 1865). Her sense of her self-control — her power over
her emotional responses to Embree's actions — is significant to Tennessee's ability to adapt to his behavior. Though
she explains that she "dislikes for Beulah to read . . . that her
Papa caused her Mama to feel angry (October 3, 1865), by
revealing her self-control and distancing herself from her
emotional reaction in her rational discussion for her daughter, Tennessee can alleviate some of her anxiety about her
relationship with her husband. She reveals that she has the
ability to resist the doctor's critiques by controlling her
responses to them. She can also redefine her behavior for
her daughter and resist the implication that she does not *try*
to govern her temper, as she states clearly and proudly that
she *does* do so.

Though she does admit to responding to his comments, Tennessee rationalizes her anger, explaining: "I think the Dr's [accusation] was unjust and consequently it kindled my anger though I ta[l]ked calmly with him" (October 3, 1865). Still, to show her self-control Tennessee chastises herself "for this revelation" of feelings. By the close of her journal entry and after suitable attention to the day's contents, Tennessee reveals the cause for her anger, as well as the emotional tension in her marriage. She describes Embrcc and his daughter Nattie as "very much alike in disposition both *cold* hearted toward others." Additionally, she explains "the Dr — says "he loves to be loved *but not to love*" (October 3, 1865; original emphasis). The details about her marriage and the doctor's personality are more elaborate than those in Henrietta's diary, and they clarify what both Embree marriages may have been like. Indeed, the connection between both women is particularly striking at this point. Each has offered a description of Dr. Embree's attitudes toward love. According to Tennessee, the doctor's cold-hearted nature contrasts sharply with her own desire for companionship. While Henrietta crafted her writing to reveal her emotional understanding without graphic details of her physical life, Tennessee's pointed details show, without overt explanations of her reactions, her emotional and physical life. As she reveals her personal life to her daughter, Tennessee also uses her writing to teach herself and her daughter emotional discipline to cope with Embree's abuse, using her justifiable anger in the very controlled response that she captures in her journal.

However, maintaining this emotional control is quite laborious and Tennessee's strength wanes, as she soon relates: "sometimes I feel as if I had nothing in life to live for"

(October 12, 1865). Echoing Henrietta, who commented that she had "never felt so little like living" (64), Tennessee shows the continued strain of her relationship within the pages of her journal. Though she addresses her daughters, Nattie and Beulah, it is clear that the journal has become the companion with whom she can discuss her marriage. She explains her despair in describing her feelings that she is "encompetant for [her] task in life" because of her own personality trait, which is, notably, a positive one: "my nature is very independent but I try to suppress such feelings so that I may better do my duty to my Husband who was always such a 'petted child'" (October 15, 1865). By defining her husband's behavior, whatever it may be, as a result of his being a "petted child," Tennessee displaces blame as well as accepting it, finding cause and comfort for his strange behavior in his parenting. A similar pattern in Emily Hawley Gillespie's diary is noted by Suzanne Bunkers. As Gillespie documented her husband's abusive behavior, she "validated her refusal to accept his behavior as a 'normal' part of married life" ("Diaries and Dysfunctional Families" 224). This strategy is a significant and successful coping mechanism. As Miller and Porter found, "to the extent that a battered woman is inclined to blame herself for her husband's violence, she will be comforted by any information that suggests that the cause of her partner's violence resides with him" (144). By blaming her own "independent" nature, Tennessee discovers a way to reinforce her own strength. Miller and Porter note this strategy as a successful adaptation of battered women: "women who saw their husband's violence as a consequence" of a positive quality of their own, one from which they may have "derived pride," were "generally more optimistic about the future and [coped] better than were those women who pointed to personal qualities about which they felt negatively" (148).

As she tries to understand her husband's difference from herself, Tennessee explains the relationship and shows that she does not simply accept his ways, but tries to communicate with him about her feelings. In so doing, however, she shows her desire for the kind of companionship which the doctor cannot give her: "feel freted with Dr. E. for staying with me so little, would that my disposition was such that I should never care whether he was present or absent" (December 9, 1865). She places responsibility for fulfilling her emotional needs on her daughter, diverting her attention to her infant surrogate: "Little Beulah may you grow up and fill space in my heart that ever pleads for the attachment and affection of a loved one" (December 9, 1865). Almost repeating Henrietta's question, "why should I be dependent why not be indipendent," Tennessee tries to steel herself against the need for Embree's companionship. However, Tennessee attempts to challenge his emotional distance and effect change in his behavior. After another one of the doctor's fairly common scoldings, she explains that she confronted him and "talked to him some time about being so childish" (December 12, 1865). She adjusts to his behavior, however, by altering her responses: "I concured my stubborn nature and jumped at him and kissed him to put him in a good humor" (December 12, 1865). She does admit their differences, rationalizing, "we are very different in our dispositions" but recognizing it is *her* "stubborn nature" that must be conquered.

Tennessee's own independence, which she seems to define as a willingness to live without love or physical displays of affection, is difficult to maintain as her life progresses.

While Tennessee continues to use writing to cope with her husband's disaffection and his cold-hearted "nature" — which contrast sharply with her own need for emotional support and companionship — her attitude toward the relationship changes as she is forced to contend with her husband's critical responses and his "pecular nature" (March 16, 1866). She explains, "it is the cause of many a painful moment to me. . . . though I love him dearly he often wounds my feelings" (March 16, 1866). No longer is she immune to her husband's criticisms, instead admitting her injury and her despair, which she cannot — unlike her anger or her independent nature — seem to control or conquer. With her confidence slowly eroding, her struggle to maintain her self-assurance weakens. Like Isabel Archer in James's *The Portrait of a Lady,* she seems different after two years of her marriage, as if "she had lost something of that quick eagerness to which her husband had privately taken exception" (323). While she had previously resisted his faultfinding, Tennessee begins to turn her criticism on herself, assuming blame for misunderstanding his nature, and responding to him with perhaps undeserved devotion. Like Henrietta who assumed her own characterological blame, Tennessee begins to find the responsibility for their marital troubles within herself. Her writing reflects a painful willingness to see herself as the problem within the relationship. If she could change, she suggests, perhaps their life would be better.

Tennessee's change is a slow process of continued adaptations and revisions, including reverting to her previous independent statements. Though she tries to adjust to his abuse with her own indifference, her anger is still apparent. She describes his childish "outbursts" and comments that he is "rather fastidious" and has "a treacherous mind." Using these angry descriptions, she warns her daughter to "learn to be mindful of all such notions that pertain to men" (April 9, 1866). With this comment, she turns collective criticism on Embree. As he has castigated Tennessee and Henrietta for the failings of "women," Tennessee now uses him as an example of the strange notions of "men," turning the characterological blame she assumed previously on her husband. After these descriptions, which serve as her protest against his "childish behavior," she shows her daughter the treachery she encounters as well as her own adaptations to Embree's continued duplicity. While she had previously expressed her anger and frustration in writing, justifying those outbursts which contrast with her self-proclaimed emotional control, she reveals how her own coping mechanisms are beginning to fail as she confronts her husband's protracted manipulation.

Describing one of the most disturbing examples of the psychological abuse perpetrated by Embree, Tennessee illuminates her husband's "treacherous mind" as well as her own declining resistance to his machinations. Prepared for and excited about the piano which Dr. Embree has purchased and delivered, to celebrate their daughter Nattie's return from the Salado Female Seminary, Tennessee enjoys the idea of learning to play: "I began to learn a little about music today feel quite desirous to know now think I would give it one years study if I can accomplish anything in that time" (April 21, 1866). It seems the perfect stimulation for her intellect, and her purposeful entry reflects her genuine self-confidence and ambition. However, she is deprived of this outlet for her interests when Embree determines to sell the piano instead. She explains, "Dr. E. has blighted my bright hopes of learning music by selling the Piano today. I believe I could make progress rapedly in that study by a little effort, (which I had thought to do)" (April 23, 1866). Unlike in her previous entries, where she expressed her anger and frustration, Tennessee now sees no point in writing about this betrayal, simply stating, "I felt somewhat vexed as he had gone to all the trouble of having it set up, but I see how useless it is to pen the varied scenes of life" (April 23, 1866). The changes in her personality over the two years of her marriage are painfully clear. She now views the expression of her anger as "useless" and even refuses to exhibit how she controlled her angry response. Avoiding any deep or disturbing recognition of the doctor's sabotage of her musical ambition, Tennessee accepts his decision and acknowledges the futility of any resistance. As the doctor's attitudes affect Tennessee's expression of her emotions and are revealed in her writing, and just as Henrietta's self-concept was altered by Embree's harassment, Tennessee's sense of herself has begun to change. While previously she tried to resist the blame he seems to push on her, finding some form of blame for his behavior other than her own failings — his "being petted as a child" (September 6, 1866) — she no longer makes attempts to explain his behavior. Again, like Henry James's Isabel Archer, "the free keen girl had become quite another person" (346).

Tennessee's changes involve her own perceptions (or rationales) of these adaptations. In detailing her changes, she attempts to remain responsible for controlling her behavior, rather than allow Embree the power to change her. After her discussion with a new acquaintance, Mrs. Thompson, with whom she "laughed and talked" about marrying widowers, whom they jokingly label as "that class of men," Tennessee reexamines her life and her marriage as she confronts her unhappiness. She explains her change to herself as well as her daughter, "I have [been] ever since I married so *foolish* about Doctor Embree that I never have taken my thoughts from the channel of devotion long enough to improve my mind in any thing (compositionaly speaking)." (September 18, 1866; original emphasis). While she had previously "thought he would appreciate such manifestations of love," she now finds that her self-described "foolish" attempts are "an empty buble to him" (September 18, 1866). In her attempt to take control of her life, she explains, "to night I concluded I would attempt to train my nature to suit his feelings and try in the future to occupy my feeling different." Again, Tennessee takes control by adapting her behavior to his, changing herself to suit the situation. Her need "to be loved in an affectionate way," she hopes, will be filled by her own daughter whom she "would teach . . . to love me in that manner" (September 18, 1866). Their relationship is clearly, and disquietingly, influenced by Dr. Embree's coldness. Tennessee details the disturbing effects as she writes, "I can now win [Beulah] to do most anything by manifestations of grief, she will kiss me many times and show how fondly she loves her Mama" (September 18, 1866). This disturbing pattern of emotional blackmail shows Tennessee's own adaptations to the isolating environment of her marriage. Powerless to change Embree's treatment of her, Tennessee uses her own power over Beulah to receive the emotional support she is otherwise without. Certainly the weight of these expectations must have rested quite heavily on Beulah. One can only speculate about their effect on her self-esteem.[10]

After her self-directed lecture and her determined decision to alter her behavior to suit Embree's demands, Tennessee relates the adaptations she must make. Much more graphically than she has previously, Tennessee describes his emotional abuse, struggling (and now failing) to counter Embree's continued criticism in her journal: "Doctor caused me to feel very badly tonight said his opinion of me was that I was *lazy* this hurt me very much when I know I work hard and make such an effort to please him" (October 25, 1866; original emphasis). Unlike her previous anger, now Tennessee, "hurt" by his comments, struggles to defend herself in her writing. She reminds herself here that she does "work hard and make an effort to please him." Her efforts do not seem to help, as she writes the next day, "I feel almost envious of the happiness of others when there seems so little comes my way" (October 26, 1866). Slowly, she adapts to his criticism of her physical and intellectual failings, reinforcing his comments with her own. As she writes, "I sometimes think [the doctor] does not consider me very intelectual" (January 17, 1868), she admits to her "unfinished" education and pins her hopes on her daughter to fulfill what she now views as her own failings: "how I wish my little daughter I was thouroughly educated, I hope all unfinished in my education may be complet in thee" (January 17, 1868). No longer does she feel superior to her husband, as she did early in her diary, but now she shows how his criticism has diminished her self-assurance. She had shown herself to be an avid and critical reader in previous entries and though she feels some pride in her reading, Tennessee now begins to view herself as not very intellectual, reflecting the comments of her external critic. In confronting this saboteur, she finds in her diary a place to keep her self-esteem from plummeting by reminding herself of her independent educational achievements: "most or near all of my knowledge is self acquired for this I deserve credit, I have read a good deal and been a close observer" (January 17, 1868). However, it is clear that the value she places on independent inquiry matters little in facing the doctor's continued criticism.

In her attempts to ensure a better life for Beulah, Tennessee, though she previously encouraged her daughter to find a husband who was not a widower, now begins to encourage alternatives to marriage with far more pointed comments. She writes more adamantly, "be sure never to marry a widdower for I would not wish you to pass through what I do in life" (July 27, 1868). In what seems to be an increasingly threatening environment, Tennessee's advice becomes more urgent. Rather than marry, Tennessee advocates emotional and financial independence. She writes: "I wish you dear child to be well-educated so that you can be prepared to support yourself in future life when your mother can no longer care for you" (July 30, 1868). As she writes this advice for her daughter, Tennessee moves from warning her daughter against marrying a "widower," to encouraging her daughter to be independent and self-supporting. Whether Tennessee herself wishes she had never married, much less married a widower, is only speculation. However, Tennessee clearly intends for her child to receive the education she did not and, through this education, to avoid her mother's experiences and her dependency.[11]

The reasons Tennessee encourages her own daughter's independence become painfully clear as she continues to struggle to comprehend the violence within the household. She graphically relates the doctor's abuse of three-year-old Beulah and tries to explain his actions to herself and her daughter.[12] She writes, "Beulah acted very ugly in church. . . . her Pa left and brought her home and whiped her all the way and continued to do so after we got home" (October 8, 1868). Tennessee attempts to alleviate her own guilt about this beating and to differentiate her own ideas of discipline from her husband's, explaining "she is so hard to conquer she needed the whipping though I dislike to see her whipped so severly" (October 8, 1868). She also notes the doctor's contrition: "the Doctor seemed sorry for her, brought her a little candy this evening" (October 8, 1868). This brief episode is detailed further in an entry one week later. Once again, it is through Beulah's voice that Tennessee is able to elaborate the details of Dr. Embree's violence. She is also able to elaborate on her own defense of Beulah, perhaps writing to clarify her efforts to protect her child, and to present her *physical* as well as her written resistance to Dr. Embree. After several entries detailing Beulah's slow recovery from Embree's beating, Tennessee writes of her visit with her friends, Captain and Mrs. Harris, and Beulah's description of the beating: "she told at the table about how her Papa did when he whiped [her] he 'drug mama [by] her silk dress and said her mama you shant whip my child so' Capt. Harris laughed at her" (October 16, 1868). Clarifying her child's explanation, Tennessee writes that she "explained to him about what we did, when her Papa was whiping her and I concluded he had whiped her enough and tried to take her from him and he would not give her up, this is why *he draged me in the silk dress*" (October 16, 1868). She repeats the episode to Embree who, apparently unconcerned, also "laughed about it" (October 16, 1868). Once again Tennessee writes somewhat more assertively after she receives supportive female companionship. Instead of denying the abuse within her household, Tennessee elaborates and explains publicly what happened in her home.[13] These connections with other women may offer Tennessee additional insights into her relationships. As with contemporary battered women who received counseling, Tennessee's communication with other women may have "reduced pluralistic ignorance (the belief that one's problem is particular to oneself), thus reducing attributions to the self as a problem" (Dutton 120). However, it seems doubtful that Tennessee received much comfort, as both her husband and Captain Harris dismissed her story with laughter. Though it seems to have little effect on Dr. Embree, Tennessee openly describes the exchange to her husband even if his response seems to deflate any hope that he will change his actions.[14]

The last years of her journal prove that these hoped-for changes never materialize, and, as previously, it is Tennessee who changes to adapt to his behavior. As her family responsibilities increase with the births of her four more children,[15] the additional responsibilities in the mercantile store, and her new household duties, Tennessee continues writing of her difficult relationship to Dr. Embree and shows her slowly subsiding emotional strength. Rather than see the fault in her husband, she now blames herself, her own temper, and her failings for the unhappy environment around her. By the concluding entries of her journal, written approximately twenty years from its opening (1881–84), Tennessee's transformation is definite.[16] By her final entry in 1884, she still struggles to remain hopeful for dramatic personality change in her husband: "I trust by Gods help we can mold him over and that a new life will begin with us at home in maney ways" (October 19, 1884). Her hope here may be her own desire for some happy romance ending, more like the marriages of the novels she has read than her own. Her journal does not continue over their last years together. With her self-perceptions changed so dramatically during the course of her life with Embree, it seems a small consolation that Tennessee outlived her husband by twenty-three years. John Wilhoit Embree died November 4, 1895. Tennessee Keys Embree lived until 1918.

It is clear within both Embree diaries that both women struggled with the definitions Dr. Embree imposed on each of them, attempting to define themselves in opposition to his understanding and his beliefs concerning their identities. As Henry James describes in *The Portrait of a Lady*, what each woman may have envisioned as "the infinite vista" became instead a "dark narrow alley with a wall at the end" (373). Their paths in marriage "led rather downward and earthward, into realms of restriction and depression to where the sound of other lives, easier and freer, was heard as from above, and where it served to deepen the feeling of failure" (373). At first, each woman employed her writing in her efforts to resist her husband's defining. Each wrote to an audience as she attempted to present her own sense of herself which differed from Embree's interpretation. Henrietta continually reiterated her own efforts to succeed even though she was continually "blamed." Tennessee insisted on her own interpretation of her actions as she explained and created herself for her daughter. While writing seems to be a successful adaptation to some extent, Henrietta and Tennessee Embree show how ineffectual writing can be as a weapon against continued personal assaults. As their husband, the other whom they strive to resist, continues to confront them, both begin to adapt to his criticism. Slowly each incorporates the outside criticisms into her own writing and turns these critiques on herself. Henrietta slowly accepts the faults with which she has been labeled, and Tennessee slowly gives up writing, also accepting what seems to be the inevitable conclusion that writing can only help so much as a defense mechanism. Faced with a definition continually imposed by Embree, these women negotiate changes to their own identities and alter their own interpretations as they are influenced by their husband.

However, each woman does not completely give up writing. In fact, each woman continues to resort to writing, even though she seems to accept and agree with Embree's verbal abuse. Henrietta, afraid and facing her own death, writes to express what she cannot express to Embree. Tennessee, though sporadically, continues to write and criticize her husband's habits, even though she admits she feels powerless to alter his behavior. For each woman, though writing may have been a rather weak and eventually ineffectual weapon, it is still a weapon of resistance. Writing to their children, each could attempt to present her own story even as she herself changed. In her study of Hannah Cullwick and Arthur Munby, Liz Stanley cautions critics to remember "power is neither simple or unchanging [and is not] a 'thing' which, if one person has 'it,' then another person has not" (178). It is instead "a process effected and affected, by a multiplicity of means" and one to which feminist scholars must pay careful attention. In these two diaries, the power each woman holds is her own self-representation and self-revision. As they write, they are able to "exchange position of object for the subjectivity of self-representational agency" (Gilmore 12). While their power may be tenuous and fragmentary, they "assert the right to speak rather than be spoken for" (40). Gilmore posits while "the writer may stand to gain little leverage against a particular institution or condition" by writing her autobiography, "it may be enough to reconfigure the grounds of contention as ideological"

(40). To comprehend the significance of each writer's self-representation, Liz Stanley suggests our contemporary understanding is linked to "an act of comprehension on the part of the writer, and thus a dimension of *how* she understands, using *what* evidence, and *when* in relationship with her subject/s" (178). As readers, to understand her, we "similarly select, omit, emphasise according to a framework of comprehension, but necessarily proceed from what the writer provides" (178). Applying Stanley's kaleidoscoping lens to these diaries, we can see that our interpretations depend on how we look, what we look at, and when we look. In the case of these diaries, recognizing their writers' small triumphs, as well as their changes, in this continued struggle, is significant to continued understanding of women's autobiographical writings. Henrietta's and Tennessee's diaries provide evidence of their own struggle for self-definition and autobiographical agency as well as their inevitable adaptation to their husband's behavior.

THREE

"When shall this warfare in my soul be ended?"

Negotiating Private Conflict and Public Crisis

ᵒThen Judith raised her voice and cried "Praise God! O praise him! Praise God, who has not withdrawn his mercy from the house of Israel, but has crushed our enemies by my hand this very night. . . . Look," she said, "The Head of Holophernes, O the Assyrian commander-in-chief! . . . The Lord has struck him down by the hand of a woman!" . . . And Ozias said to Judith, "My daughter, the blessing of God Most High is upon you, you more than all other women on earth; praise be to the Lord, God who created heaven and Earth, and guided you when you struck off the head of the enemy commander! . . . You risked your life for our country when it was faced with humiliation. You went boldly to meet the disaster that threatened us, and held firmly to God's straight road." All the people responded "Amen! Amen!"

THE BOOK OF JUDITH

The apocryphal story of Judith encapsulates a view of women and political action which challenges more traditional interpretations of women and the public sphere, and offers scholars an appropriate allegory for women's involvement in the American Civil War. Judith, a devout and respected widow, asserts her own personal power to affect the political events of her nation. Rather than passively accept her position as participant (or victim) in the political conflict which endangers her city, Judith asserts her own influence and succeeds in halting the siege as well as the war which would inevitably follow. Proclaiming that she will "do a deed which will be remembered among our people for all generations," Judith sets about to end the siege of her city and defeat the Assyrian invaders (8.32). Before her public adventure begins, Judith prepares privately, asking God to "give to me, widow as I am, the strength to achieve my end" (9.9–10). Braced by her personal ritual, Judith dresses for her public performance, changing from her widow's weeds into "her gayest clothes . . . so as to catch the eye of any man who might see her" (10.3–4). Thus costumed, she and her maid travel to the Assyrian camp where she announces her surrender in order to save her city and nation. Captivated by Judith's words and beauty, Holophernes welcomes her and prepares a feast in her honor. Judith continues her performance until Holophernes is drunk with passion and wine. After all the servants withdraw from his tent, Judith's real drama begins. Standing over the Assyrian leader, Judith draws Holophernes' own sword and, praying again for strength, she beheads him. Without their leader, the Assyrians retreat and are defeated by the Israelites. Reinforced by her own private rituals and her private "self," Judith enters the public sphere, enacts her performance, and creates a public self which has significant influence on the present and future of her country. It is through her action, her public performance as well as her private self, that her own country is saved from disaster. In the "presence of all Israel" (16.1), Judith sings, "The Lord Almighty has thwarted them by a woman's hand. It was no young man that brought their champion low; no Titan struck him down, no tall giant set upon him; but Judith, daughter of Merari disarmed him by the beauty of her face" (16.6–7). After joyous months of celebration and though "her fame continued to increase," Judith returns to her private life, does not remarry, and continues to live in her husband's house. The Book of Judith closes with a testament to one woman's power over the political world: "no one dared to threaten the Israelites again in Judith's lifetime, or a long time after that" (16.21–25). Like Judith, Confederate women during the Civil War asserted their own personal power, entered the public sphere with their cultural assumptions concerning appropriate feminine behavior, and attempted to influence the outcome of the political crisis through their own public and private endeavors.

In the highly segregated social environment of the American South, women were confronted by war which brought on a "crisis of identity" (Faust, *Mothers of Invention* 6). The "radical shifting foundations of social power" challenged women's — especially slaveholding women's — self-definitions (7). However, these women did not abandon the comforting structure of their world-view. In fact, as Faust suggests, their commitment to "the fundamental values and assumptions of their prewar world ultimately enabled them to contain much of the change war seemed destined to inaugurate" (7). By remaining somewhat true to their prewar conceptions of identity, based extensively on the public/private structure of gender relations in the nineteenth-century, these women, though "inevitably shaped by the revolution they experienced . . . nevertheless struggled to resist its full import by striving to impose their vision and their self-interest on the circumstances of a changed world" (7). As LeeAnn Whites suggests, the "ultimate recognition of the patriarchy actually lay in the willingness of Confederate women to go one step beyond [their] very domestic roles, to transcend their own privatized domestic place in the name of the basic patriarchal principle that animated it" (*Civil War* 40). Thus, rather than challenge the patriarchal notions by which they defined themselves, Confederate women began to apply these notions to the public sphere, redefining their roles as well as their understanding of public/political events. While the war effort gave Confederate women a "rare opportunity" for acceptable political involvement, they could enter the public sphere because "their privatized domestic pursuits [which] were now thrust into the center stage were not in violation of their subordinated domestic status" (Whites, "Civil War" 15). While most women "were careful to heed admonitions to remain within their appropriate sphere. . . . in the course of their actions they would also redefine themselves" (Faust, *Mothers of Invention* 23). Within the context of the war's outbreak, LeeAnn Whites notes, "critical events in the course of women's lives [such as the loss of a child] . . . became [of] central, public and political concern" (*Civil War as a Crisis in Gender* 38). Thus the public/political/masculine realm began to be understood in more "private" terms. As Faust articulates, during this crisis of national identity, women became "acknowledged creators and custodians of public as well as domestic culture in the wartime South, exercising their power over communal sentiment in a variety of ways" ("Altars of Sacrifice" 177). Applying their domestic duties to the public sphere, Confederate women did not alter their thinking about themselves, but rather maintained a gender identity consistent with the cultural understanding. Rather than become more "public" themselves, these women privatized, or domesticated, the public sphere as a means to comprehend their excursions into the more political events of the war.

The influence of an individual female citizen was not a foreign idea to women of the nineteenth-century, because women's virtue "constituted a national resource" (Smith-Rosenberg 174). Women's spheres of influence extended out from the center of their domesticity and piety to influence the larger culture. As Jane Tompkins has shown, even the world of sentimental fiction espoused women's powerful influence on the culture, because it was based on the "theory of power that stipulates that all true action is not material but spiritual; that one obtains spiritual power through prayer; and that those who know how . . . to struggle for possession of their souls will one day possess the world through the power given to them by God" (*Sensational Designs* 151). The cultural work of sentimental fiction was to influence the public sphere with the values of the private/female sphere, and the "welfare of the nation . . . depended on the virtue of the individual citizen" (156). Similarly, Nina Baym has argued that in antebellum America, the concept of Republican motherhood was directly based on women's political influence over the national character: "what was carried on in the home related crucially to one's own country, for it was nothing less than forming those beings who

. . . would preserve or bring down the republic" (277). The private sphere of home was not alienated from the public but directly related to it. The home "was neither a retreat from nor the alternative to the polity — it *was* the polity, the place where the state and the people became one. . . . [W]omen at home could be charged with considerable political and national resonance" (277). Thus, the eventual danger of women's suffrage was not the damage to the "female character" but rather the loss of nonpartisan political training in the home. If women could vote and participate in partisan politics, the "primary meaning of republicanism as a suprapartisan preserve of domestic values would be forgotten" (293–94).

The ideology of separate spheres gave white middle-class women significant moral responsibility over public events. As Elizabeth Fox-Genovese notes, women "developed the notion that they served as custodians of a special private morality" and "set about applying their moral standards to the larger world" (79–80). Rather than alter their self-concepts to adapt to the changes occurring in the Civil War, women applied traditional gender relations which "linked the individual woman to the larger world" (Fox-Genovese 372). Thus, the gender roles that "defined [a woman's] place in the world" and "through which she was encouraged to realize her identity" remained comfortably in place (372). According to Fox-Genovese, these gender conventions "delineated an order that confirmed the women's deepest sense of who they were" (372). From their position of moral authority, women extended their "jurisdiction into the public and hitherto exclusively male realm by using the 'domestic' role" as a means of gaining power and influencing the public by the "exploitation of their domesticity" (Clinton

41–42). Especially during wartime, women were encouraged to become "civic" beings (Elshtain 9) and apply their domestic claims to the public realm. Empowered through the discourse of "civic virtue," wherein a woman's patriarchal/domestic virtues are applied to a larger public realm, women were able to become the "author[s] of deeds" (Elshtain 93). Still, these deeds were the domestic/private deeds at which women excelled — food production, caring for the sick, and mothering. These duties formed the foundation of many women's organizations which arose out of the war efforts on both sides of the Mason-Dixon line, and which would inevitably, as Anne Firor Scott suggests, "prepare women for their great leap forward in the postwar years" (59). However, with the onset of the Civil War, the expectations for women extended beyond their gendered private sphere. Not only did their private sphere influence the public sphere and the national character, these women also had to — and were even encouraged to — enter the public sphere and perform public duties that had previously been performed by men. Drew Gilpin Faust has argued that, in the South at least, the most "fundamental and essential political act" became a public responsibility of women ("Trying to Do a Man's Business" 198). With the departure of most of the male population, women became responsible for the direct exercise of control over slaves, and thus became the enforcers of a political system which relied on the paternalistic division of the sexes.

Judith Butler has suggested that "when a relevant culture that constructs gender is understood in terms of a law or set of laws, then it seems that gender is . . . determined and fixed" and culture "becomes destiny" (8). In terms of the American Civil War, the concept of women's gender was based on a highly patriarchal and paternalistic culture in which

> women's clearly defined roles as women . . . consti-
> tuted an integral aspect of [the perpetuation of a
> slave-holding system].
>
> Women who challenged these prescribed roles
> threatened the foundations of slave society, of Chris-
> tian society, of all civilized society. Women who
> accepted them inevitably accepted limitations. In
> return they gained protection against their weakness,
> respect for their particular excellence and an unchal-
> lenged status as ruling ladies. (Fox-Genovese 287)

With the onset of the Civil War, this paternalistic culture was threatened, as were the very definitions of gender that had been applicable in the South. When the cultural definition of a gendered destiny is thrown into confusion by the collapse of that cultural/social system, how do women confront or adapt to the accompanying alterations to their behavior expectations? As Butler posits, "if the 'inner world' no longer designates a topos, then the inner fixity of self and indeed, the internal locale of gender identity, become simi-larly suspect" (134). In the case of the Civil War, gender identity becomes suspect as the public and private spheres merge, losing the distinctive gender divisions established by the antebellum social order. Butler argues that "gender is an identity tenuously constituted in time, instituted in an exte-rior space through a *stylized repetition of acts*" and that this "requires a conception of gender as a constituted *social tem-porality*" (141). According to Butler, "the action of gender requires a performance that is repeated" and, in the repeti-tion, is "a reenactment and a reexperiencing of a set of

meanings already socially established" (140). If the very performance of gender was altered, and suddenly a woman was
expected to perform not feminine but masculine, not private but public, duties, how would she maintain an identity
based on her own sense of herself as a private/feminine
person? How does she "repeat" the performance that
signifies her own gender, and her own embedded sense of
self, even as she performs the duties of another gender?

In my previous chapters, I have discussed how women
have used writing to maintain their sense of self as they
experienced variations in place and encountered changes in
their personal lives. In this chapter, I will examine how two
women, confronted with large social change which alters the
fundamental structure of the society in which they have been
identified and by which they have identified themselves, reinforce their sense of themselves as private women while they
performed public duties and braved social transformation.
Lizzie Hatcher Simons and Cornelia Noble, both residents of
Texas during the Civil War, used writing to support a private self engaged in public performance and to comprehend
the public situation in a private manner, through private/
personal writing. As Joanne Braxton suggests of Charlotte
Forten Grimké, diaries "represent a retreat from potentially
shattering encounters" and offer "a place of restoration and
self-healing" (256). Similarly, Nancy Walker argues that the
tone of autobiographical writing by Emily Dickinson, Alice
James, and Virginia Woolf is determined by the tension
"between personal and public," and that through letters and
diaries, these women found "a way of defining themselves
and presenting themselves to a world outside the self" (278).
I suggest that, like these other women writers, Simons and
Noble used their private writing to reinforce their sense of

themselves as private and to extend their private influence into the public sphere of the war.[1]

The Civil War did encourage many public performances by women. Lyde Cullen Sizer discusses the skillful use of gender ideology by the celebrated female Union spies Pauline Cushman, Rose Greenhow, and Belle Boyd, in "Acting Her Part: Narratives of Union Women Spies." Faust suggests that women who performed nursing duty were seen as "not truly women, but in some sense men in drag" ("Altars of Sacrifice" 186) and has also examined the popular stage representations known as *tableaux vivants* in which women acted publicly, and scandalously, on the stage to raise money for the Confederate cause (*Mothers of Invention* 26). Women also performed public duties that were much more personal and private, duties that their husbands and brothers left behind when they joined the Confederate forces. While performing masculine tasks, these women wrote to support their public performance by maintaining their private selves in their diaries, and to identify with the public crisis of the war. In this way, their private selves became the supporting cast, so to speak, as each performed her public duties. By identifying the public conflict of war with familiar domestic, personal, and private experiences, these women blurred the boundaries between public and private even as they reinforced their sense of self as private women. Thus, though they performed public/political/masculine roles, they reminded themselves of their domesticity and their private/personal/feminine domain by writing and transforming the alien public sphere with personal and private interpretations. During the war, their performance was necessary but temporary. Rather than re-structure their identity to become public "like men," they became public like women, personalizing the political events so they could perform without altering their sense of self and continue to espouse the ideology of their culture.

In her journal, written August through December of 1862, Lizzie Hatcher Simons confronted the social changes that accompanied the Civil War, while she lived in the coastal region of Texas.[2] Living with her younger sister, Kate, and sometimes her Aunt Jud, Simons faced a domestic situation altered dramatically with the departure of her husband. Simons' living arrangements may have been typical as Faust has noted that, in the South, the mobilization caused by the war brought many women into different living arrangements as they relocated to safer places. Women moved back into their own family households or had other women move in with them so that they would be less isolated during the conflict (*Mothers of Invention* 33–34). On August 31, 1862, Simons writes of her regret at not having kept a diary "during the past year, the most eventful of my life" which she refers to as "the most marked by 'sarking care'"(3). Her diary reveals an important bond with her community and her attempts to manage her own now public duties. She opens her journal with a discussion of her new, more public, and less domestic exertions, recognizing the social shift in gender expectations as she explains, "[t]he following is a list of *unladylike* jobs I have to perform during Maurice's absence whilst in the army" (1). The "unladylike jobs" Simons catalogues express her creative ingenuity as well as her physical strength as she performs the tasks expected of her. Clearly there is no choice as these are jobs that she has *had* to do:

> When Kate and I returned from Dr. Woolfolks we
> had to unharness the horse and put the buggy away.

At another time some one who borrowed the buggy left it out in the street and Kate and I had to roll it into the buggy house. found a tub with the bottom out. went to put it in and found the whole thing fell to pieces after working a long time on it got it together and the bottom in, but the lower hoop was gone and had to send to the shop and have another put on — had a calf tied near the front gate whose mother was delinquent after a while the cow came. I undertook to take the calf down to the lot. it almost jerked me to pieces. the only way I kept it off was by winding the rope around a tree I got it to the back fence and got Aunt Miley to help me *put it over* and thus got the cow and calf together, but I was sore for three days and jerking the ropes thru my hands almost skinned them — found the ash hopper leaked badly. went to work dug out all the ashes tore it to pieces and made a new one — went down and tried to make a corn trade with Mr. Sanford but failed because he asked me too much — dug around the rose bushes and grape vines — one of my best tubs taken to water the calves, fell to pieces went down to doctor it, pressed Willie into service we worked at it an hour after bruising our fingers and getting over heated got it together but one little piece of the bottom brought it into the house, laid the case before Milam. . . . he took off the lower hoops and soon got the piece in made a churn dasher — put handle in hammer made a corn trade with a negro went out nearly 10 o clk at night to see it measured. — put in window glass. — swung a gate Put new fossil in cistern. (1–2)

While she admits to the unfamiliar and definitely gendered tasks she has undertaken, Simons catalogues those she has successfully completed or attempted, reinforcing her ability actually to perform these unconventional acts. Despite the "unladylike" aspects of these physical activities, Simons seems less uncomfortable with her performance than proud of her ability to accomplish these rather alien duties. The length of her list and the continued explanation of additional tasks which involve physical labor, creative thinking, and business acumen, all reinforce what she has been able to accomplish. Though she "fails" in her attempts to make a "corn trade," she succeeds in not giving up "too much" in the bargaining. As well as accomplishing her chores, she also recognizes that they are outside the realm of appropriate gender behavior. Even as she admits that she can and does perform them, these tasks still involve a performance. She does not challenge the nature of these "unladylike" actions but rather adapts her performance to accomplish her duties. Simons copes gracefully even if she publicly displays seemingly disgraceful and unfeminine behavior. And all of these jobs are performed *very* publicly — chasing a cow, putting away the buggy left in the street, dealing with slaves and overseers as well as tradesmen. Her new public duties certainly seem to her very different from her previously private domestic duties, but she balances her performances with her private recognition of their temporary nature and the "unladylike" nature of her accomplishments. Thus, she is not unladylike, the jobs are, and even so, they must be performed while her husband, who "went to war October 8, 1861," is away (2).

As well as the physical tasks she must undertake, Simons also engages in the political discourse of the time. Commenting in her journal on September 20, 1862, she presents

herself as politically aware and particularly wary of the relia-
bility of the news: "Lee and Stonewall Jackson have routed
Pope and McLellan and are marching on to Washington oh
how glorious *if true*" (14). She also expresses a high level of
political sophistication as she interprets her community's
response to the news of September 24: "such splendid news
had come that Washington is taken oh if it was only true but
it comes in too doubtful a form to be relied on much tis
amusing to see how its [received]" (16). Astutely, she interprets the variety of reactions: "the croakers say 'its impossible I know its not so' the hopefull, 'I hope its so' the
enthusiastic 'I know its so'"(16). Her humorously circumspect response to the information shows her careful consideration of the public news. While she may certainly be a
private person, she is not naive and refuses to be taken in by
the rumors, even as she hopes they are true. Her entry into
the public sphere of political debate is countered by her
discussion of the more feminine duties she continues to
administer. Though seemingly domestic and of the private
sphere, her actions take on a political meaning as she strives
to have some influence on the conflict. To resolve her feelings of idleness, she and the other women of her community
resolve to "go to work in earnest and make clothes for our
dear ones" (17). As Mary Chesnut notes of this very popular activity, "the knitting mania *rages*. You never see a woman
without her needles are going" (143). Within this community of women, Simons begins to recognize the political
influence of her domestic actions. Rather than enter open
public debate in this situation, Simons and the other women
turn their domestic duties into political actions, even making public display of their domesticity: "we think of nothing
but our plans of sending clothing to our dear ones in the

army. I even knit on my way [to town]" (18). Knitting so publicly counters her previously "unladylike" performances and exhibits her commitment to her private sphere and her domestic duties as well as the significance of this private action to influence public events. This open parade of womanly action may displace any discomfort she found in the exhibition of other more masculine performances. Even though she has had to perform unladylike duties, she still maintains her true identity as feminine. While still proud of the strength and ingenuity that she had previously cata-logued so carefully, the public display of her femininity reinforces her sense of self as of the domestic sphere. This candid demonstration is not "performance," but the *real* expression of 'feminine' identity. For Simons, "masculine" duties were performed while her own "feminine" tasks were much more indicative of who she believed herself to be. While contemporary scholars might consider both gendered tasks as performance and equally constructed by cultural contexts and ideology, Simons comprehends her femininity as essential and significant to her own sense of self. Writing of her enthusiasm for and commitment to knitting, she reminds herself of her 'true' nature just as she has shown others her femininity. George Rable has suggested "the war strained traditional definitions of gender by testing long established customs. . . . [b]esides sewing banners, cooking meals or listening to stump speeches, few women had played a role in the political culture" (135). By their overt exercise of femininity, Simons and the other women in her commu-nity *were* playing a role in the political culture. Their very legitimate display of the gender ideology, on which the south-ern paternalistic social order was based, served as the appro-priate political action for the women and also reinforced their sense of identity as they were confronted with masculine duties that seemed to belie the antebellum gender order.

The success of this displayed femininity is short-lived, and the women's domestic efforts to support those in the public sphere of the war are threatened. By October 3, Simons reports, "Mrs Coleman came in and threw cold water over my plans" (19). She tells of a neighbor who, having just returned from the army, discourages the women's efforts remarking that "our men don't need anything that what we would send would be in the way, that they would throw them away, that he took socks for them and had to bring them back and offered some of his shirts and they wouldn't have them" (19). Simons' attempt to assist the soldiers is thwarted, and her efforts to extend her domestic influence into the public realm seem wasted. Still, she attempts to focus on what she as a woman can do for the men: "oh if I could only know what to do! the idea of their being in that cold climate poorly clad is distressing" (19). Without this sense of purpose, Simons finds no way to direct her energies toward any material show of support. Though it seems that her feminine support may be pointless, Simons continues to knit socks and sew shirts for her husband. Even if she cannot support the Confederate army, her domestic duties to her husband can be maintained despite his distance from her. Denied any feelings of greater political contribution, she still has a personal connection to the crisis because her husband serves the Confederacy. Her support of his endeavors ultimately reflects her support of the larger cause.

Just as Simons publicly displays her domesticity and envelops the public sphere in the private, she extends her personal connection to the political cause beyond her familial circle, identifying not only her own relevance to the war through Maurice, but also the other members of her immediate community. Increasing the boundaries of her familial identifications to encompass even non-family members, Simons expands her private sphere to incorporate much more of the public: "one y'r to day [October 8] my lov'd husband left home and friends to embark in his country's cause oh how sad is the retrospect! . . . what will the records of another year unfold!" (20). To counter her emotional turmoil and her anxiety about her influence on the public sphere, she strives to recognize that her isolation seems minimal in context with the tragedies others have suffered: "deep gratitude ought to fill my heart to day for many of those brave ones who left us one year ago today, have pined away and died in hospitals, while some have fallen on the battle field and others have told of weary hours in northern prisons" (20). Her small private sacrifices and her separation from her husband are minuscule when she compares her own experience to that of others' much more public and permanent sacrifices. Though she may not feel as she thinks she "ought," she reminds herself that her own domestic sphere, though altered by the war, has not been permanently changed. Her own husband is "blessed with health" and is progressing up the military ranks with his promotion from lieutenant to major (20). The personal and private connection of larger political crisis is not only through her individual ties to Maurice but is also reflected by the dramatic changes occurring in the neighborhood surrounding her. The community's casualties merge with her own as she extends her responsibilities to the more public world. Despite her desire to perform her duties with "brighter hopes and better resolutions" (23), she notes the influence of the war on her private life and its impact on her domestic sphere. Recalling the pleasant scenes over which she had previously presided, she writes, "I felt sad to think how different twas [branding time] a y'r ago. What a great lot of them we'd have to dinner whilst branding here. now some are on the battle field far away, while others, hale, hearty young men full of life and animation are now filling 'strangers graves'" (23). Remembering these private and personal moments links her to the more public and political world. The troops involved in this conflict are those very people she had cared and provided for in the previous year. Her contact with these "hearty young men" makes her relationship to the larger political cause much more personal and familiar, even familial. So even though she may feel alienated by the changes in her domestic duties and her inability to influence the public sphere, she reinforces her link to these men as she remembers their roles in her domestic life. Her own reaction to the unsettled conditions of her life, disrupted by political strife, results in even more personal emotional repercussions.

Just as her response to the public events of war generates a personal domestic memory, her own private events now reflect the public turmoil surrounding her. Simons recalls not just the loss of her husband to active military duty but also the loss of her own mother: "all in the house are asleep, but I who am sad sad just 1 yr ago [October 16] this night our loved Mother left us . . . how vividly these words rise in my head when I was all unconscious of any greater sorrow hanging over me than that my Maurice has gone from me. then those words seem burnt into my brain 'your Mother is dead'" (25–26). These two isolating moments, the departure of Maurice for war and the death of her mother, are now intertwined just as Simons' personal and domestic life is now embroiled in the public and political sphere of the Civil War. Recalling her emotional pain, she begins formulating an understanding of her fear and sense of loss caused by the war. Still, as she privately grieves these public/private losses, she continues her own performance for her own public — her sister and aunt — as they cope with the Federals' late October assault on Port Lavaca, Texas. While she explains that all is "gloomy and sad" and that her sister and aunt are "almost sick with fear," she has a responsibility for a certain public performance. In this case, she must adopt a particularly comforting and feminine role, very much like the mother she herself seeks. She writes, "I feel very very badly but try to be cheerful to reassure others" (35). In this frightening atmosphere, she connects the emotional turmoil of the physical attack with the loss of her own mother: "amid all the confusion and trouble cant help thinking of one y'r ago today [October 31] when I heard of my darling Mother's death oh the anguish of that day and the many days that succeeded" (35). Thus, in the midst of political and public "confusion and trouble," it is the private and personal loss of her mother, perhaps the primary domestic figure in Simons' own life, which she recalls. This recollection may perhaps represent in some way the disruption of Simons' own comforting and domestic connections. Thrust as she is into a violent public conflict, she may long for the comfort she found in her own domestic and familiar sphere just as she desires the comforting familiarity of her own mother. As in previous entries, her references to her mother's death appear in her darkest moments *and* in connection to the war. Perhaps it is the struggle to remain cheerful during these moments of fear and anxiety that recall her own displaced reaction to her mother's death or her psychological need for her mother's consoling presence. Her mother's death seems the deepest grievance she has previously experienced, and it is this response she uses to name her fear at this moment. Thus, she defines her own psychological state, brought on by her apprehension about Maurice and her necessary public performances, by direct comparison to the most painful moment she has previously experienced, making her mother's death a defining emotional metaphor for her experience of the war. Simons links this emotional memory to the political turmoil of the war and uses this connection to comprehend her own position in these complex political events.

Simons' private adaptations to the public sphere continue to occur as her role in the political drama of her country develops. After the battle at Corinth (in late October), Simons receives the desperately awaited news from her husband and brother in the Second Texas Regiment, and her private letters become public as she disseminates the information to her community. As she had previously done, Simons personalizes the results of this political action, detailing the names of those who were killed or injured in the battle: "Lt. Haynie killed shot all to pieces, Gen Bolyn mortally wounded, Capt Goff Col Rogers and Gen. Moore killed sad sad record Willie Sanford came to hear of Jon. [he is] among the missing Dr Wells came to hear the news" (32). Thus the familiar and familial names serve to bring the distant events into her own domestic sphere. These seemingly public events have private repercussions, and she thinks "continually of the desolate hearts and homes in our midst" (32). Using her private letters to share her information and also applying her feminine duty to care for those injured, now those injured by this information, Simons again expands her domestic duties to include the public sphere: "great many came to hear my letter. Mr Haynie's servant came, I wrote the poor old man a note told him his son was kill'd. . . . Mr Allen called and many others" (33). The domestic space of her own home becomes a public gathering place as she shares her information with her community. Not only does Simons share the personal news, she also engages in political news, discussing the "great excitement about Gunboats being at Lavaca" (33). Just as her private letters have a kind of public duty, her own domestic space now becomes a forum for public and political discussion. The public and private spheres converge in the intimate contexts of her letters, diary, and home — all private spaces — and are now very much within the public sphere.

As her domestic spaces become more public, her own home is threatened by political action as the war draws nearer: "great excitement about the yankies reported that they've taken [Powderhorn]" (33). Simons avows her own significance in confronting the danger. Writing of her friends' decision "to run when the feds come," Simons asserts "*I* say I'm going to stay at home" (33). Her own political action, to defend the domestic space that is her home, directly reflects her own political consciousness. She *will* stay home, and this action *will* have a political influence. Just as her public display of domesticity reinforced her commitment to the gender ideology of the Confederate cause, she will now defend her home with her actual physical presence, not just symbolic action. Her very defense of home and her announcement become a public display of her very political will. Now even the private spaces are of public consequence and have become arenas for political struggle; even from her own home on November 1, she writes that she can hear the "heavy firing" on the port at Lavaca (36). This public presence results in more performance by Simons as she notes again that her aunt and sister are "almost sick with fear" (36). While Simons had previously asserted her strength to defend her own home, she now writes, "I feel miserable but try to be cheerful on account of" Kate (36). Just as she had done previously, Simons reveals her own private anxiety to her journal while she tries to perform cheerfully for those around her. Her writing supports this public performance by allowing the private expression of her own fear and misery as she tries to cope with the new and more personal threat of war. While she tries to face the public threats of actual military invasion with the courage of her convictions, Simons faces another manner of invasion, one that threatens her family and herself in more personally violent ways. On November 2, she writes "northern papers insinuate theres to be an awful insurrection through the south so Bro F tells me" (36). Unlike her response to the potential Yankee invasion, she reacts with more fear and anxiety, writing that she can "hardly keep tears back the idea of an insurrection is horrible to me cant get it out of my mind" (36). Certainly her personal fears of rape and murder as well as the threat from an interior source — her own slaves — have more influence over her than the political threat of invasion. Now she, not the idea of the Confederacy, could be the target of a very personal, violent attack and direct assault on her gender identity. She is now made aware of her position as a woman in her culture. Simons no longer has the paternalistic male social order designed to protect her, and which encouraged her own domestic dependency. Though "Lavaca has not fallen yet," Simons faces important decisions about her own security and that of her domestic sphere. As before, her neighbors encourage her to flee, and she writes, "[C. Dibrell] urges us to leave offers his wagon and carriage and help move us. . . . Coy C says [Kate] must go home with him" (36). Confronted with the frightening changes to her family circle, she explains, "Im almost distracted dont know what to do whether to stay or buck up and leave. . . . M[ilam] killed beef afraid to pickle much think we'll have to leave soon" (38). With the increasing personal danger of insurrection, Simons loses her sense of strength and becomes more personally and emotionally isolated. Her domestic circle of family is disrupted when her sister Kate does depart, and she seems to lose even her impetus for performance: "[Milam] went off just at twilight a lonely hour anyhow L[izzie] and I felt very lonely and I felt sad. . . . no letters for any one, no news thats good. my soul is sad these times" (38–39). Isolated from her supportive domestic sphere, Simons must confront the public sphere with other private measures. As she seeks further understanding of her position within the political crisis, she tries to find comfort in her faith and writes about symbolic choice between public and private interest. Choosing to read her Bible rather than a Chicago newspaper sent by her husband, she finds her selection "Providential," as her reading enables her to perceive the value of her personal experience even if she feels that the "little crosses of life seemed to bear heavier on me than usual" (43). Remarking on the reading "so suited to my case," Simons notes simply: "1st Cor: 10th and 13. I felt comforted" (43). In the poetic imagery of these passages, Simons finds comfort in a metaphor that enables her to comprehend her position in the political events. Despite her

feelings of idleness, her reading choice offers her an understanding of the importance of her efforts. Within 1 Corin-
thians 13, Simons discovers an illustration for her own
significance in the political conflict. Her private reading
supports her public self and also suggests the power of her
particular influence over the public sphere. Within the bib-
lical passage she finds an answer to her helplessness with the
reassurance that her own 'love' is the greatest of her powers,
even more than her faith. Her anxiety about Maurice's suffering and her own inability to comfort him with tangible
objects or to sacrifice herself, to "deliver her body to be
burned," is relieved by recognizing that, despite her fears,
her support is a significant contribution. She is also reassured that although the purpose of the current circumstances is unclear, she will some day "understand fully." Like
Judith, she responds to the threats of public invasion with
private prayers that strengthen her and encourage her own
action, even if her action is seen as minimal.

Simons' own fears of the private/public merging again
take shape when she confronts the possibility of a slave insurrection. By November 29, the rumors which were circu-
lating previously concerning a slave uprising have come to
fruition: "I hear too of troubles in H[alletsville] with the
negroes several were hung" (49). This very close threat, more
personal and even physically closer than the Yankees at Lavaca,
again reinforces Simons' gender identity and her vulnera-
bility as a white woman. Though she tries to displace her
own fear by writing, "I know that makes K[ate] feel badly"
(49), clearly Simons' own isolation and fear is equally disturbing. Though she expresses concern for her sister's well-
being, concern which relates directly to her domestic sphere
and her role as caretaker, she struggles to deal with her own

fear through the private expression of her faith. As Judith prayed for strength to carry out her public performance, Simons prayerfully writes to sustain her own spiritual sense and to cope with the ever increasing threats of physical violence: "they say a plot has been discovered in which negroes from Halletsville to Lavaca are implicated God deliver us from the horrors of an insurrection" (49). She seems to find some personal strength in this private action as she explains, "oh I feel sad sad to night. Anxious about Bro D uneasy about K gloomy about our country, oh what would become of me if I could not go to my kind Heavenly Father with all these troubles?" (50) In the private action of writing, the private action of prayer, Simons finds support for her public self as she confronts the personal changes the political actions cause. The potential of a direct personal assault because of the political environment puts her private sphere in direct contact with the public sphere, and, to cope with these political public threats, she turns to private/domestic reinforcements. These reinforcements do not always arrive, as she explains, "when I allow myself to think, I am sad, sad, and gloomy" (50). Thus her public performance now keeps her from pondering her situation too closely. While she had previously supported her presentation with private actions, the public performance now takes all her concentration, so that she is distracted from more dangerous private thoughts. The support for this altered public exhibition is still private faith, however, and her domestic ideology remains intact even if it seems less effective than previously: "my only hope is in God and I do feel that I would be sunk in despair if I had not that hope. . . . God help me in this dark hour, for surely the clouds are dark and lowering" (51–52).

With the threat of invasion, as well as insurrection, comes another political assault on Simons' sense of herself. On December 28, she reports that "the brute Butler is to [head] the army invading Texas" (64). General Benjamin Butler was infamous for his "General Order No. 28" which declared that any woman who showed "contempt for any officer or soldier of the United States . . . shall be regarded and held liable to be treated as a woman of the town plying her avocation" (Faust, *Mothers of Invention* 209). His direct application of southern gender ideology to reinforce his occupational control of New Orleans was extremely successful, driving directly "to the heart of the ambiguities in white southern women's identities" (209). Butler confronted the public display of domestic scorn with a direct reference to their femininity. These ostentatious exhibitions were not to be seen as reflections of "ladylike" behavior, and thus his command returned women to what society considered their rightful place (Faust 209–13). For Simons, this threat on her domestic sphere and her public identity as feminine is very powerful. She explains, "[w]e have fresh incentive now to flee from our homes and seek safety anywhere when the highest officer is a greater brute than any private" (64). Butler's application of gender ideology is not a compliment to the feminine sphere but an insult to the Confederate women who have supported the public cause of the South with their private actions. And the potential of his arrival in Texas threatens both Simons' public and private selves and spheres. In the face of this threat, Simons turns to her private ritual, writing and praying: "He has said 'call upon me in the day of trouble and I will deliver thee'" (64). Thus, she asserts, though tentatively, her personal/private sensibilities as she faces this new public threat.

By the close of her journal December 31, 1862, Simons has turned again to the private ritual of writing and prayer to support her own public performance during this assault on her cultural conception of the world. The Civil War itself confounds her public and private roles, merging the spheres as she is forced to manage both rather than one. Still she manages the public through continued reliance on her private, domestic duties. Simons recalls the public influence on the domestic situation, remembering "many happy homes have been desolated, so many loved ones have parted never more to meet on earth" (68). She also reminds herself that her own domestic connections remain intact, explaining, "my loved ones are spared and I still have hopes of being clasped in the arms of my loved one, still have hopes of seeing my own kind brothers and sisters" (68). As she writes, she expresses her ambiguous responses to her circumstances: "I feel that I ought to be filled with gratitude to God for having still spared their lives" (68). Despite her ambivalence, she reinforces her belief and her own private sense of the world as she again links her domestic circle to the larger political events of the war. This connection makes her own private ritual one of public importance as she invokes the power of God to influence the outcome of the political action. She writes, "I know his loving kindness is great and I do desire above all things to glorify his Holy name. and now the last leaf of my journal is written and the last hour of the year is passing. and in this solemn hour when all around me is silent I invoke a blessing Gods richest blessing on my husband, my child and my brothers and sisters" (68). This final prayer shows that she strives to perceive her connection to the dramatic political events in terms of private domestic sphere. It is also through the private ritual of prayer that she finds a role and purpose more clear than through other, more tangible, contributions to the public arena. Her personal connections to the public sphere, through her public display of femininity early in her journal, to her private invocations for divine influence over the public crisis, maintain her understanding of herself as of the private/domestic/feminine sphere, even as she confronts the public/political/masculine sphere in which she must perform.

Simons' public displays of domesticity and her efforts to assert her own personal influence over the political conflict are paralleled in the diary of Cornelia Noble. Also writing in Texas during the Civil War, Noble begins writing prior to the Civil War in 1860 (on her journey from California to Hays County, Texas) and closes in 1864, before the conflict's end, on the birthday of her son Woods.[3] For Noble, the Civil War crosses the boundary between public and private spheres and becomes an even more personal conflict than it was for Simons. Noble's impassioned and deeply pious interpretations of the sectional conflict represent not only the culturally coded conception of the divine righteousness of the Confederate cause, but also reflect her own crisis of faith triggered by her move to Texas and reinforced by the public strife. She views the political action through the lens of her own personal crisis, adopting the war as a personal indicator of her religious commitment, and measures her own spiritual failings against the success or failure of the Confederate troops. By identifying with the conflict so personally, Noble exerts her private control over the public event and applies her piety, not only to her own religious reform, but to the reform of the nation. While Simons adapted to the public world and reinforced her sense of self as of the private world through public and private displays of domesticity, Noble reinforces her sense of self as of the private by the continued exercise of her piety, another key ingredient in the feminine sphere. She extends her control of herself and the private realm into the public, and, in some instances, insists on the significance of this private, personal conflict to direct the public and political events of the war. By continually paralleling her own crisis with the public conflict, Noble personalizes her connection to the public sphere by exerting influence through her piety and her own self-control.

Like Simons, Noble's actual personal connection to the conflict is through her husband, Moses, and it is when she must face the possibility of this very personal link to the war that she begins to elaborate on her interpretations of the conflict. When Moses suggests that "his country need[s] his services" and asks if she is "willing for him to go" (December 29, 1861), Noble writes of how intimately this crisis will affect her: "[h]ow can I bear to see him go and I and my children be left with strangers and I might never see him again?" (December 29, 1861).[4] Her husband's commitment to the public world and her own commitment to the domestic domain seem in direct conflict. Her personal isolation is now linked to the political situation and, though she is "troubled" by Moses' question, she begins to adopt the political crisis as her own, interpreting the larger political situation through its direct impact on her and her direct impact on the conflict. Upon receiving news from relatives in Virginia concerning the possibility of English involvement in the war over the arrest of southern ambassadors Mason and Sliddell, Noble writes, "in a rather cold and indifferent state of mind. . . . Well, I hope and pray for peace, but I rather think the North will accede to the demands of

England, though it may be very humiliating to them as a nation" (January 19, 1862). While she seems to be relatively uninterested in the political news, when she addresses her own personal crisis, she applies the same language she used to describe effects on the North, to describe what she feels she must learn to achieve greater spiritual fulfillment. While the North may be "humiliated" in being forced to acquiesce to the demands of England, it is humility that she herself may need to learn. She reasons, "it seems to me that the Lord has brought me to this country [Texas] to teach me humility and to show me what was in my heart. . . . I must learn to yield my will to that of the Almighty" (January 19, 1862). Just as Noble feels the North must accept England's demands and be humbled, she also must "learn to yield" her will "to that of the Almighty." Her parallel imagery here also reveals how she may think that it isn't just England that the North must accept. Indeed, the Confederate cause itself may be linked to much higher powers than national ones.

Linking the Confederate cause to divine providence is not simply Noble's own idea. The religious fervor generated in the Confederacy was stirred by many popular publications. Noble, reading her *Churchman* periodical newspaper, discovers a public call for such personal intervention in the political crisis. She writes that the "Churchman calls on the people to humble themselves and pray earnestly to God to deliver our country from our enemies and turn all there counsel against us into foolishness" (January 19, 1862). Appropriately, the request is for humility, just the inner quality Noble herself feels she lacks. This call reinforces her connection to the crisis through her own private ritual as well as her private conflict. This public call builds Noble's sense of power over and responsibility to the political events, and she also adopts the war imagery to illustrate her own personal crisis. Within a month of this entry, Noble's identification of the public predicament with her own private struggle is complete. As she relates the news of a Confederate defeat in Kentucky, she writes, "I don't feel I have made much progress in the Divine life this week. . . . When will I learn wisdom? When shall this warfare in my soul be ended? — Not til death end my earthly existence — till then. I must fight and watch and pray and great will be thy reward if I am faithful" (February 22, 1862). Just as the Confederate forces have not made progress, neither has Noble. In fact, the Confederate defeats seem directly related to Noble's spiritual failings. As they are defeated, so is she. The private and public crises are now linked inextricably in Noble's writing. The warfare in her own soul is the warfare in the nation. Confederate defeats are her defeats as she struggles to maintain her own faith by her expressions of piety. After she exhorts herself to "fight and watch and pray" for her great reward, she explains another Confederate defeat, at Roanoke Island in North Carolina: "our troops fought bravely and did much execution, but the Federals came in such overpowering numbers that they had to yield and many were taken prisoner" (February 22, 1862). This surrender, much like her own, is only a result of superior enemy forces. As she must fight and watch, so the soldiers "fought bravely and did much execution," despite their ultimate surrender. Like Noble herself, these soldiers resist until they can no longer sustain the effort. Like the soldiers, she will submit to spiritual defeat only after great resistance and struggle. Linking her inner turmoil to the political conflict, Noble heightens the significance of her own personal crisis of faith and her private sphere's influence on the public sphere. Like Simons' public display of very domestic knitting, Noble's display of personal piety, even if it is within the pages of her journal, is still a display of her personal influence over the political sphere.

When Moses joins Wood's Cavalry in San Marcos, Noble's personal connection to the war is solidified and her religious fervor intensifies. Her zealous expressions of piety are directly related to Moses' enlistment but refer to the larger spiritual failings of her nation. Now she has even more responsibility to the Confederacy, as her own husband must be protected by her prayers as well as her actions. To influence the national situation, Noble writes, "I observed the past week as a time of fasting and prayer I believe all these troubles and afflictions have come upon us because of our sins" (March 10, 1862). She delineates the sins of her nation: "we have become deeply corrupted — pride — fullness of bread, ingratitude — violence, profaneness blasphemy and oppression reign in our midst" (March 10, 1862). To alter the consequences of these sins, Noble claims some personal responsibility, explaining fervently, "I feel that unless we repent our sins that he will bring along yet heavier afflictions upon us. I feel as if the sword of His wrath was suspended o'er our heads but we are now feeling some of its heavy strokes" (March 10, 1862). By her own actions, she exerts her own personal power over the national conflict, "so I fasted and prayed to Him to sanctify to us our afflictions to pardon our sins — to give us grace to humble ourselves under his Mighty hand and to Turn away from us the rod of his wrath" (March 10, 1862). Noble's personal relationship to the war is exemplified in her actions. As she writes, "*I* feel unless *we* repent" and then, "so *I* fasted and prayed" (emphasis added), her influence over and relationship to the public sphere through her own private actions, as well as her own private rituals and beliefs, is made explicit. Through her presence, she influences the political crisis. And it is through the lens of her own spiritual crisis that she sees the need for public change: "Our country is in an awful state and is I think growing worse daily. The Lord is permitting these things to come upon us for some wise purpose. For humiliation for one thing I believe . . . We need humility and prayers full of faith" (April 1, 1862). As she has stated several times previously, she feels that she must learn humility and humble herself before God and accept his will. Thus she applies her own crisis, her own need, to the larger conflict and heightens her own significance to the public sphere.

And for these prayers she seems to be rewarded. She *has* been influential in the war and her reward is the Confederate victory at Corinth. As victory is recorded in the public conflict, she reinforces her own private victory in recognizing her dependence on God and her acceptance of his grace. In one of the most impassioned entries of her journal she soliloquizes the triumph in her acceptance:

> To God giver of all good things belongs the praise.
> . . . I feel my dependence on God — that I myself
> am incapable of doing anything to please him —
> that it is only the gift of his grace that I can do any-
> thing acceptable in His sight. the life I live now, I
> live by faith in the Son of God. My hope — sole and
> whole hope is in Jesus — in the 3 mercies of his
> sufferings, death and resurrection, the full and suf-
> ficient atonement which he has made not for my

sins only, but for the sins of the whole world. I loath
and abhor my sins and long for a deeper work of
grace in my soul. I feel myself to be a most unworthy worm of the dust and that it is only by grace I
stand through faith in our Lord Jesus Christ. (April
20, 1862)

Just as Simons sought a sense of purpose through her work
for the soldiers, so Noble shows her sense of purpose in
her prayerful entry. As she thinks that the country "needs
prayers full of faith and humility," she offers her own
prayers to show her humility and faith in an effort to affect
the struggle between Union and Confederate forces. Her
personal offering of humility serves as her contribution to
save the soul of the nation. However, her humble and effusive prayers are also an indication of her own triumph. She
has succeeded in accepting that "only through the gift of
grace" can she do anything "acceptable in his sight." Thus
her expression of humility is actually a boast. As Jane
Tompkins has suggested, this submission to this higher
power "gave women another ground on which to stand, a
position that, while it fulfilled the social demands placed on
them, gave them a place from which to launch a counter-
strategy against their worldly masters that would finally give
them the upper hand" (*Sensational Designs* 162). This form
of submission is a "self-willed act of conquest of one's own
passions" (162), and "submission becomes self-conquest
and doing the will of one's husband or father brings access
to divine power" (163). Like the characters in sentimental
fiction, Noble, "by conquering herself in the name of the
highest possible authority[,] . . . merges her own authority
with God's" (163). Thus, Noble's acceptance is triumphant,

a personal victory for herself and her country. Her recognition of her faith and humility is intertwined with the public conflict, and as she expresses her piety, she controls the outcome of the political actions. In some way she is stating "I *am* the crisis," not to blame herself, but rather to exert her own power over a situation in which she has previously seemed powerless.

This symbiotic relationship does have its consequences, and a personal and Confederate victory in April does not mean continued success. By August, Noble's intimate relationship with the public sphere has produced profoundly different results. She writes of her own spiritual failures and her desperate attempts to submit to what she perceives as the will of God and the temptations of the "Adversary" (August 31, 1862). Berating her lack of commitment, she explains:

> tho' my conscience bears me witness that I have made efforts to [be a consistent follower of the Lord] yet I feel I have come far short of the mark. In the first place I feel I am in a sad and lukewarm state. . . . I see so many failures and above all I have not a lively sense that I have done all to please my God — I have some fears this evening, tho it may be a temptation from the Adversary, that what I do is merely get to a happier state and to escape punishment due . . . to my sins — but my heart repels the accusation. (August 31, 1862)

In the wake of these dark admonitions, Noble writes, "the Federals have possession of a large portion of Va and are committing many outrages on unprotected women and children" (August 31, 1862). Just as her own spiritual successes were linked to the Confederate victories of April, Noble now links her own spiritual failings to the Federal victories. Her personal temptations by the "Adversary" are public victories by Federal troops. Because she has asserted the divinity of the Confederate cause previously, this must, of course, mean that the Federal troops are sanctioned by the "Adversary," and their "many outrages on unprotected women and children" reflect this unholy alliance. Her own temptations "merely [to] get to a happier state and to escape punishment" are indicative of the public failures of the Confederate troops. Admitting her "unworthy prayers," she continues, "I feel that I am too light and too easily influenced by others. . . . I want to have a constant and lively sense of the awfully sublime majesty of God and his Goodness" (August 31, 1862). Confronted by the Confederate losses, she has increasing difficulty in seeing "the majesty" because of "the outrages" in Virginia.

When Confederate victories again occur, she interprets these as signs of God's allegiance to the South; however, she seems to have lost the fervor of her previous entries. With news of a victory at Harper's Ferry and reports that the Confederates "are carrying the war into the enemies country," Noble tries to regain her confidence in the divine actions of her nation, writing, "if these things are so we ought to thank God for it all we could not win unless our efforts were blessed by him" (October 5, 1862). The very underpinnings of Noble's cultural understanding, the divinity of herself and her nation's cause, are slowly eroding. Rather than restructure her interpretation of God or herself, Noble begins to reconstruct her conception of the Confederate cause: "I have many fears for our dear country tho we just heard of the success of our country under Price"

(October 16, 1862). Once again she relies on the very familiar and very personal doctrines she has espoused earlier in her journal: "Oh that as a people and as individuals God would give us grace to repent of our sins and turn to the Lord with our whole heart" (October 16, 1862). In expressing her convictions, she again exerts a personal and private control over the public and political conflict. In support of her ideology, she observes "a day of fasting and prayer" and explains that she has "had neither eat nor drink today" and has been "trying to be humble and devotional" (November 30, 1862). Still, she continues, "I see so much coldness and worldliness in me today. I have felt very far off from God but I long to draw near . . . to him" (November 30, 1862). Her direct connection to the public crisis is again made clear as she ties her distressing failures to the sufferings of her nation: "our poor bleeding distressed country. May God have mercy on her — for it looks as if his arm alone can save her — but his arm is powerful" (November 30, 1862). Her own distance from God and her country's distance from God are parallel. As she longs to draw close to God, so too does she pray for "his arm" to save her country.

In addition to her own private devotions, there is again a public call for her personal intervention. Just as *The Churchman* had called on citizens to pray for the outcome of the war, now the political leadership of her own state directs a petition for private intervention and influence over the conflict. On the third of August, 1863, Noble's private convictions are rendered public by the Texas governor's appointment of "a day of fasting." Noble, in hearty agreement, asserts, "if there were ever such a time that called for fasting and prayer surely the present is such. I feel it to be such" (August 3, 1863). As Noble confronts what she views as her friend's lack of patriotism, Noble again makes her public display of piety and fervor an indication of her control over the public sphere. She writes, "Mrs. Young thinks there is no necessity in leaving off work and she may fast as acceptably as I do before the Lord but I feel like the eminent danger our country is in calls for unusually strict fasting, humiliation before God and repentance for our sins" (August 3, 1863). Her commitment to the Confederate cause as well as her devotion to her religion do not alter in the face of public defeat. As the South suffers, she suffers, and while she had previously believed that Confederate victories were ordained by God, she has also continued to maintain that Confederate defeats are a result of God's displeasure, not with the social structure of the South, but rather with the Confederates' inability to accept God's significance in their lives and to humble themselves before his power. She reinforces her commitment to her religious beliefs and resolves "to strive to live a more humble holy and devoted life — I want to have earnest devotion and an eye single then to the glory of God this year, if I live for I see that I lacked it sadly last year" (January 1, 1864). Despite the uncertainty of her future, Noble confirms her trust in God, affirms her faith, and accepts the future. Her submission is not failure, but triumph over the fear and panic of those less faithful: "the future is hid from me and I know not what is to become of me but I am resolved to trust in the Lord" (January 1, 1864). Though the circumstances of the future seem bleak, the outcome of the war uncertain, and her own private influence of the public sphere dubious, Noble maintains her socially constructed and acceptable identity as reverent and constant to her faith. Throughout her journal she has reinforced her private influence over the public conflict as she has made the public crisis her own. Elaborately detailing her devout efforts to influence the public sphere through her own acceptably feminine and domestic industry, Noble emphasizes her own significance in a conflict that seems to isolate her from all she finds familiar and "true." Through her own expressions, she maintains her own significance and her position of power as a moral authority in a failing culture.

Both Simons and Noble assert their own control over the political situation by the exercise of familiar domestic and feminine duties. As their society is restructured, and each is faced with threats to their personal and cultural understanding of themselves, these women apply the power most acceptable to them, that of domesticity and piety, to alter the public conflict. Even as they are faced with a radical alteration in their duties and the foundation of their social identity as feminine, Simons and Noble do not seem to alter their sense of self, but rather assert their significance as women and domestic participants in the political arena. As these women write of their experiences during this dangerously transitional time, they reinforce their familiar concepts of self rather than alter the foundation on which these selves are constructed. Even though their social order is undergoing massive upheaval and their future is extremely uncertain, Simons and Noble resort to the powerful familiar structure of their cultural understanding. Even though the performance of public/political/masculine duties challenges their identities as women, as they attempt to control the public crisis through their expressions of domesticity and piety, they reinforce their own sense of themselves as of the domestic/private/feminine sphere. Writing these expressions of their femininity and their moral authority over the public conflict, these women reiterate the very patriarchal and paternalistic social order on which they rely for their identities. And, as the Confederate cause begins to fail, they continue to exert familiar interpretations to comprehend its collapse rather than alter the foundations of their socially constructed identity.

FOUR

Something in Particular
Writing, Journals, and the Evidence of Presence

I feel that I have had a blow; but it is not, as I thought as a child, simply a blow from an enemy hidden behind the cotton wool of daily life; it is or will become a revelation of some order; it is a token of some real thing behind appearances; and I make it real by putting it into words. It is only by putting it into words that I make it whole; this wholeness means that it has lost its power to hurt me; it gives me, perhaps because by doing so I take away the pain, it gives me great delight to put the severed parts together. . . . From this I reach what I might call a philosophy; at any rate it is a constant idea of mine; that behind the cotton wool is hidden a pattern; that we—I and all human beings—are connected to this; that the whole world is a work of art; that we are parts of the work of art. Hamlet or a Beethoven quartet is the truth about this vast mass that we call the world. But there is no Shakespeare, there is no Beethoven; certainly and emphatically there is no God; we are the words; we are the music; we are the thing itself.

VIRGINIA WOOLF, "A SKETCH OF THE PAST"

T hroughout her journal, Sarah Morgan refers to the significance the act of writing has for her psychological management of the Civil War and the destruction of her society and culture. She ponders the loss of her pen, which she considers her "greatest consolation under all afflictions." Without the writing, she explains, "I really think I would fall victim to despair" (216). So committed is she to her writing that she refuses to send her journal to a safer location despite the threat of Yankee invasion and the possible violation of her intimate thoughts. With the Federal troops approaching her home in Baton Rouge, she writes,

> My earthly possessions are all reposing by me on the bed at this instant, consisting of my guitar, a change of clothes, running bag, cabas, and this book. For in spite of all their entreaties, I would not send it to Clinton, expecting those already there to meet with a fiery death. . . . They tell me that this will be read aloud to torment me, but I am determined to burn it if there is any danger of that. Why I would die without some means of expressing my feelings in the stirring hour so rapidly approaching. I shall keep it by me. (436)

Fortunately, Sarah Morgan's diaries survived the war, the invasion, and the repeated calls for their destruction. In her writings, we have access to Morgan's thoughts during her experience of war and we have her own commentary on the significance her writing played in her life during this time period. Some diarists make such explicit comments about the act of writing; for others, simply the existence of their writing must speak to their commitment and use of this action in their daily lives. As Judy Simons argues, the mere existence of women's diaries reveals bourgeois women's desire "to validate themselves through literary expression" and also shows the "emotional and imaginative investment" women made in maintaining their journals (253).

In my introduction, I suggested that by examining the act of writing and by carefully attending to the moments of being represented by the individual journal entry as well as the whole work — what Rebecca Hogan identifies as the "principle of parataxis" in the diary form (101) — scholars could begin to comprehend the significance of the writing moment as a means of creative agency for women confronting the external circumstances of their lives. In the case of the six women I have discussed here, writing did provide a substantive conduit for self-assertion as they faced what were sometimes seemingly insurmountable situations, and it is through their continued use of writing that they retained some form of psychological control of their existence. Robert Fothergill has argued that the "function of the diary is to provide for the valuation of [self] which circumstances conspire to thwart" (82). For these nineteenth-century women, not only the physical and psychological circumstances of their lives have thwarted their efficacy; the patriarchal culture in which they exist has conspired to erase their significance and sometimes even the very evidence of their presence. In each entry of a woman's journal we have a moment when a woman, despite what she may write and how she may depreciate her journal's significance, takes a pen in her hand and writes "I am." In the masculinist tradition of autobiography, the autobiographical 'I' has traditionally been based in patriarchal perceptions of an independent, autonomous, and male self. This creates a certain paradox for women who choose to write "autobiography." Sidonie Smith explains the "Catch-22" of women who desire to write auto-biography in this patriarchal tradition:

> patriarchal notions of women's inherent nature and consequent social role have denied or severely pre-scribed her access to the public space . . . and pro-foundly contaminated her relationship to the pen as an instrument of power. If she presumes human identity . . . she transgresses patriarchal definitions of female nature by enacting a scenario of male self-hood. As she does so she challenges cultural con-ceptions of the nature of woman and thereby invites public censure for her efforts. If she bows to the dis-cursive pressure for anonymity, however, she denies her desire for a voice of her own. (7–8)

When a woman chooses to write "I am," she must cope with the female conventions prescribed by her patriarchal culture which complicate her "struggle for individuality" with the "culturally prescribed norms for female identity" (10). Still, when a woman does write, whether she adapts to or defies culturally prescribed norms, she does still voice aspects of her own existence denied by the larger patriarchal culture. These writing moments are an addendum to the Cartesian model, which becomes, in this instance, "I write, therefore I am." Women writing are asserting something more like "I write, therefore I am *too*" in the face of circumstances and a culture which may tauntingly suggest otherwise. In a culture which suggests certain norms for female identity, including modesty and the acceptance of personal insignificance, a woman who writes about herself, even if she adopts patriarchal construc-tions of women, makes herself significant enough to chal-lenge the prescribed norm.

Though seemingly disparate, the six women whose journals I have discussed here wrote under very similar conditions. The instances of their writing occur as each woman faces an external threat to her own sense of self and her understanding of the significance of her presence. And in each case, the women wrote to control their identities — how they perceived themselves to be — rather than allow circumstances or others to alter their sense of themselves. These women adapted their self-understanding when external circumstances seemed fixed, or they altered their external circumstances, through their personal interpretations, to reflect their sense of themselves when they needed to maintain a comforting and fixed identity. Confronted with personal dislocation, Abigail Jane Scott and Jean Rio Baker recognized themselves in alien places, reinforcing their own sense of themselves during their overland journey west. They were figuratively saying "I recognize this place, therefore 'I' am not misplaced." Faced with a lifetime of psychological abuse by the man they each had chosen to marry, Henrietta and Tennessee Embree wrote as they struggled to understand themselves against Dr. Embree's continued derision and aggression. In their disturbing alterations, these women at first write "I am not as he says I am," but slowly adapt because he certainly will not change. It is easier for them to control their own sense of themselves and change who they perceive themselves to be, even if these changes are very disquieting and self-destructive. Encountering the massive social and cultural upheaval caused during the American Civil War, Lizzie Hatcher Simons and Cornelia M. Noble wrote to maintain their own sense of self as the society in which they defined themselves altered and restructured. As their worlds fall apart, they write to recognize themselves even though their world changes. They seem to be writing "I do not know this world, but I do know who 'I' am and I will continue to know who 'I' am even as my world changes."

While it may be tempting to suggest that these women wanted to be remembered for their suffering, careful examination of their texts suggests otherwise. As Fothergill suggests, "the constant process of rendering a version of oneself to the silent audience of the diary plays a significant role in the psychic economy of the diarist, and the tenor and the selective presentation of material reveal that role at least as clearly as the diarist's explicit statements on the subject" (82). Rather than suffer in silence, or detail only their difficulties, these women wrote, perhaps unconsciously, to establish their presence as well as to leave evidence to someone — family, friends, or future readers. While they might, as both Simons and Noble do, glorify the gender ideology of their culture, in doing so they asserted their own power, however limited, amidst even the most disempowering social constraints.

In each of these journals, these women wrote for themselves and others. Even though diaries are generally regarded as personal and private, they stand as evidence of their writer's corporeal existence in their current incarnations as now public documents. In addition to writing for themselves, these women wrote to make known to others that they existed, that they were present. In this writing moment, these women were declaring their existence to their future readers, whether they be family members or some unknown future reader. Constructing their own identities in their journal pages, these women made themselves for themselves and for their own constructed audiences. Sharon Hymer has explained that the shared diary may be an attempt to "project a cherished aspect of [self]" so that the eventual reader might gain a more "complete understanding" of the writer (17). Despite their difficult circumstances, these women wrote to proclaim that they had a significant presence, even if the external conditions of their lives seemed to imply their absolute insignificance. Scott and Baker were faced with dramatic and alienating conditions on their journeys west. The very geology of the West reinforced their insignificance as they crossed the continent. Confronted with the harsh and unsympathetic natural conditions of the Overland Trail, Scott and Baker used writing to announce their interpretations of these new places and signify their own existence. Henrietta and Tennessee Embree were challenged every day by the intimate presence of Dr. Embree and his continued harangues and character assaults. The person to whom both of these women were bound under the religious and legal strictures of nineteenth-century society continually sought to alter their own identities, replacing their individual sense of self with his concepts of them. Even though both women do seem to alter their sense of self, they continue to write, telling what they know and how they know themselves. Henrietta writes to her daughter, Nattie, and her sister, Jen, and Tennessee writes to her daughter, Beulah and, eventually, her four other children, to identify and to explain themselves within their writing. Their journals speak for them when they are altered and silenced by Dr. Embree. Simons and Noble write to confirm their sense of who they are and to claim responsibility in a political conflict which expressly denies their physical involvement and relies on the disempowering gender ideology endemic within their culture to reinforce the paternalistic social order of the Confederacy. By writing, these two women claim control and influence over a conflict which challenges the very foundation of their socially constructed selves. By writing, all of these women were collecting themselves together and being under circumstances that made their being questionable and, in some cases, seemed actively to prohibit that being. As Lynn Bloom suggests, "through the act of writing, the author not only composes her own character, she moves that character to center stage, becoming the principal actor in the drama of her own story" (32). By writing, all of these women claimed existence and presence during situations which continually questioned the actuality and the significance of both.

Philippe LeJeune has indicated that his own purpose for exploring the journals of young women in nineteenth-century France is to "circumscribe and understand" the "collective writing adventure" and to "decode the meaning of those texts within their contexts" (112). This collective writing adventure is what links these texts together most effectively. While scholars have argued extensively that the diary is the feminine form of autobiography, or is the definitive female autobiography, or the "real" voice of their writers, I suggest that perhaps a more profitable approach to journals is to examine these texts as writing moments and strive to comprehend how and when women have written, privately as well as publicly. Rebecca Hogan has suggested that in diaries the "principle of parataxis works . . . on the level of the larger diary structure in relationships existing from entry to entry, from month to month, from year to year" (101). She argues that the "paratactic form" can be examined from two perspectives; one is the "even metonymic flow of events and entries" which creates the "sense of continuity required by diary-keeping" (104); the other is the "series of related items, events and entries without the use of connecting links" which creates the "sense of discrete, separate entries also required" by diary-keeping (104). We can also extend this parataxis paradigm to include the links between actual diaries themselves, and even to our own writing about them. With my own writing, I compound the significance of these writers and present my text as further evidence of their existence to those who may not know of them. Their personal writings, imbued with their own significance, now acquire additional significance in their transformation into my own public and scholarly document. My own writing moments in this study originate in the writing moments of these nineteenth-century women. If they had not authored their texts, I would not have been able to author my text. Thus, it is this literate endeavor that joins these women to me and their lives to my own life as a woman who writes, trying to understand who I am in relation to the places I am, have been, and will be; the people I know, have known, and will come to know; and the world in which I live, in the past, present, and future. It is through their writing moments that I have come to write and to understand the person I myself am continually becoming.

Examining the writing moments within individual diaries as well as the intersections between diaries offers scholars an opportunity to discover the significance of journals for those who have employed this expression as a means of creative agency. While writing is only one form of agency, available to a particular and potentially narrow section of the literate population, and which has been valorized by scholarly interest in written expression, journals do offer significant insight into the lives and thoughts of their writers. As Judy Nolte Temple and Suzanne Bunkers indicate, "for some women literacy *was* life, for in their diaries they could shape and control their experiences by means of mastering language" (198).

Mastering and articulately applying language to detail, reconstruct, and interpret their experiences, these women writers have done privately what other women have achieved more publicly. While more traditional analyses of writing have focused on composition, revision, and public discourse, these private writing moments are no less a creative structuring of experience and thought. Robert J. Yinger argues that "symbolic manipulation through written language provides a means, not only for representing experience, but also for transforming it" (10). In their journals, these women I have studied have brought the symbolic manipulation of language to bear on transforming not only their experiences but also to interpret the external conditions of their lives and to assert individual control over the psychically and psychologically overwhelming circumstances which necessitate their writing. Yinger also suggests what is most compelling about reflective journal writing is "the psychological requirements of writing such as the need to structure and represent meaning that may, in fact, enable the writers to construct new meaning, or new knowledge" (16). Yinger continues, "by writing out what they know and by juxtaposing this knowledge with other pieces of knowledge to create new connections, new relations and structures come into being and new knowledge is created" (16). Applying this concept to the journals in my study suggests that the significance of their own writing may have led them to form new self-understandings as well as preserve their own sense of self against and with their new experiences. Incorporating their "new" knowledge into their own frames of reference, their own former knowledge of themselves and who they were, offered these women an opportunity to adapt creatively and assert their own interpretations of their circumstances. Scott and Baker could control their sense of dislocation by using powerful interpretive frameworks that had previously served them in more familiar environments. Both Henrietta and Tennessee Embree regulate their self-interpretations as they adapt and resist Dr. Embree's psychological abuse within their journals. Simons and Noble assert control over political, public, and social events through the very familiar gender ideology which had previously suggested their limited sphere of influence.

Though these journals are written as essentially personal, not for wide publication, and though I have made them more public through my own writing and interpreting, they are still a process of creative agency for their writers just as more public texts have been. In *The Psychology of Writing*, Ronald Kellogg signifies the writing action:

> Meaning-making is a significant form of thinking that entails work not only in the private domain of mental experience but also in the public domain of shared discourse. We render experience meaningful by creating consensual symbols that refer to objects and events, beliefs and intentions, memories and fantasies. *Acts of meaning,* to use Bruner's (1990) phrase, define the scope of human behavior and culture. We take experiences encountered in life and imbue them with significance. We achieve this by creating consensual symbol systems that express the personal symbols of thoughts, feelings, recollections, fantasies and dreams. Through these consensual symbols we communicate with one another the significance of our experience. (203)

Thus, in the action of writing, Abigail Scott, Jean Rio Baker, Henrietta Baker Embree, Tennessee Keys Embree, Lizzie

Hatcher Simons, and Cornelia M. Noble communicate the significance of their experiences to themselves as much as for any future readers. Interpreting their experiences, resisting and adapting to outside definitions, maintaining their own sense of themselves as they face circumstances which challenge their identities, these women applied writing to make themselves and their experiences *of consequence*.

The poet Michelle Cliff poses the question, "as women writers, does language become our mother?" and suggests the answer, "we create ourselves through language, so it would seem" (71). For these six women, created and constructed within the patriarchal social order and encountering external circumstances which threaten their existence, their journals became an outlet for self-expression and self-assertion as well as self-creation. Their creative interpretations of their experiences seem to have enabled them to comprehend and avow their presence despite cultural and physical strictures. Like stitches in an antique quilt, an image captured forever in the pose of being photographed, the hereditary recipe remembered across generations, or a family story retold to connect past with present, these writing moments are the evidence of presence left by those who wrote them. Like the chambered nautilus discovered uninhabited, these journals, as self-generated as the creature's shell, are spaces in which someone — some woman — lived and wrote. While not all women wrote, or wrote the same way, or even maintained journals, the journals that we do have — those written expressions of women who chose to write — stand as a reminder of the writers' being and as a testament to the consequence of their presence.

NOTES

CHAPTER 1

1. The Overland Trail was the primary route for emigrants to Oregon, California, and Nevada. The Santa Fe Trail served primarily as a cargo transport route to the southwestern territories. Between 1840 and 1870, a quarter of a million travelers journeyed over the 2,400-mile trail to claim free land available in Oregon and California (Schlissel 10). The trail passed through the territories of Nebraska, Wyoming, and Idaho, splitting into the California and Oregon Trails in southeast Idaho as immigrants to Oregon traveled north and California-bound immigrants traveled across northern Nevada to reach their destination.

2. For additional information on landscape aesthetics and the history of landscape, see D. Cosgrove, *Social Formation and Symbolic Landscape* (London: Coom Helm, 1984); John Michael Hunter, *Land into Landscape* (London: George Godwin, 1983); Anne Farrar Hyde, *An American Vision: Far Western Landscape and National Culture, 1820–1920* (New York: New York Univ. Press, 1990).

3. The Oregon Trail migration of 1852 was the largest and was also plagued by a nationwide cholera epidemic. Tucker Scott, reporting on his trip for the Tazewell County *Mirror*, recorded that, by May 29, the counts from Fort Kearney, Nebraska, totaled "16,279 persons, 4,777 horses, 2,905 mules, 37,883 cattle, 2,801 sheep, and 1 hog. By 14 July the figures were 23,980 persons,

7,516 wagons, 7,793 horses, 4,993 mules, 74,783 cattle, 23,908, sheep" (Moynihan 30). The Scott family traveled in five wagons with forty-two oxen, three cows, two horses, and a pony (Scott 30).

4. Abigail Jane Scott, "Journal of a Trip to Oregon," in *Covered Wagon Women: Diaries and Letters from the Western Trails*, vol. 5, ed. Kenneth L. Holmes and David C. Duniway (Glendale, Calif.: Arthur H. Clark, 1986). All subsequent parenthetical references to this diary refer to this volume. For an additional content discussion of Scott's Overland diary as well as more biographical information, see Ruth Barnes Moynihan, *Rebel for Rights: Abigail Scott Duniway* (London: Yale Univ. Press, 1983).

5. The timing of the Scotts' journey took them through Missouri two years after the Missouri Compromise of 1850. Tucker Scott's ancestors had departed Kentucky for Illinois "not only for land and opportunity, but also out of anti-Democratic and anti-slavery conviction" (Moynihan 12). These convictions are clearly present in Jenny's writing.

6. Both Tucker and Maggie maintain the journal when Jenny is unable to do so. Their observations are marked by differentiating styles. Tucker maintains financial records and exhibits a matter-of-fact attitude. Maggie focuses most of her attention on describing events and people and is also somewhat less effusive.

7. Jenny's sister, Catherine Scott Coburn, later described this young man as "Jenny's 'sweetheart' and the man she might have married had he lived" (Moynihan 38).

8. Jean Rio Baker, "By Windjammer and Prairie Schooner. London to Salt Lake City," in *Covered Wagon Women*, vol. 3, ed. Kenneth Holmes (Glendale, Calif.: Arthur H. Clark, 1984). All subsequent parenthetical references refer to this volume. For additional discussion of Jean Rio Baker and other Mormon pioneers, see *Saints without Halos*, ed. Leonard Arrington and Davis Bitton (Baker 203n).

9. Baker quotes from Milton's *Paradise Lost*, 5.153–60, which reads,

> These are thy Glorious works, Parent of good,
> Almighty, thine this Universal frame,
> Thus wondrous fair; thyself how wondrous then!
> Unspeakable, who sit'st above these Heavens
> To us invisible or dimly seen
> in these thy lowest works, yet these declare
> Thy goodness beyond thought, and Power Divine.

CHAPTER 2

1. Eighteen-year-old Henrietta Baker Embree (February 18, 1834–June 13, 1863), married twenty-four-year-old John Embree (November 25, 1828–November 4, 1895) in Kentucky, after his graduation from Louisville Medical College. Both moved, apparently immediately, to Bell County, Texas, in 1852. There they joined his brother, Elisha Embree, who had lived in Texas for two years (Embree, H. i). The couple had three children: Nattie (June 19, 1853–February 13, 1869); Mollie (September 20, 1855–February 10, 1856); and Jonnie (August 17, 1859–November 2, 1862) (Embree, H. appendix). Prior to her marriage to Embree, Tennessee Keys lived near Rutersville, Texas, then Bosqueville, and eventually Bell County, where she married. The first, brief volume of her diary, 1862 through 1864, was maintained while she lived with her half-sister, Mrs. Lizzie Giles, in Bosqueville, closing with a brief entry noting the anniversary of her marriage in 1865. The next two volumes of her diary (three to four hundred pages) begin September 25, 1865, approximately five months after the birth of her first daughter, Beulah, and close October 19, 1884. Tennessee and Dr. Embree had five children

of their own: Beulah (May 4, 1865); Russell (April 14, 1869); Harvey (July 30, 1871); Gillian (August 1873); and John Jr. (1877). When she married, Tennessee also became the stepmother to Henrietta and Embree's eleven-year-old daughter, Nattie (only thirteen years younger than her stepmother).

2. This term, developed by Lenore E. Walker (1979, 1984), refers to the psychological conditioning of women and the cycle of violence in battering relationships. Walker's cycle of violence has three phases: tension building, acute battering incident, "loving contrition" (*Battered Woman Syndrome* 95). Common characteristics of battered women include hypervigilance and the need to manipulate their environment and others (to control the likelihood of abuse), wariness, fear (learned by "living under siege"), and low self-esteem, though they perceive themselves as having high self-esteem (125–28). Children in abusive households experience shame, fear, guilt (if they were "better children" they could prevent the violence), and anxiety (Jaffe, et al. 27–28). Older children and adolescents "may take on additional responsibilities to keep the peace and provide safety for their families." Older children take on "parenting responsibilities" and "protect younger siblings during violent episodes and offer support or reassurance" after the violence. As a result they "feel they cannot leave home because they have to protect their mother or find ways to calm their father's angry outbursts" (29–30).

3. Henrietta Baker Embree, transcript of diary, Barker Texas History Center, Center for American History, Univ. of Texas, Austin; Tennessee Keys Embree, typescript of diary, Barker Texas History Center, Center for American History, Univ. of Texas, Austin. The typescript of Henrietta Baker Embree's diary is approximately two hundred pages in length. Included with the diary is a list of pledges Henrietta wrote at the end of her journal, a brief introduction titled "Aunt Hen's Diary," apparently written by a

family member, and a 1928 Belton newspaper article commemorating the 100th anniversary of Dr. Embree's birthday. The typescript of Henrietta's diary is marked by ellipses and seems to have been edited during the transcription process. The typescript of Tennessee Keys Embree's diary includes a brief introduction, which mentions the existence of Henrietta's diary, though it was apparently not in Gillian Embree's possession at the time. Tennessee's diary seems to have been meticulously transcribed by her daughter Gillian, and includes marginalia which Tennessee wrote in her own diary. Both diaries remain unpublished. I have maintained the original spelling and punctuation of these typescripts.

4. The typescript of Tennessee Embree's diary is unpaginated. I have used the dates of entries for all citations.

5. Divorce was an available option for women in Texas. The Texas divorce statute (Act Concerning Divorce and Alimony) debated in 1840 "allowed a husband to divorce his wife for a single act of adultery. A wife could divorce her husband for adultery only if he abandoned her and lived with another woman. . . . both husbands and wives could sue for abandonment after three years. . . . district judges could grant either the husband or wife a divorce for 'excesses, cruel treatment, or outrages toward the other if such ill treatment is of a nature to render their living together insupportable'" (Boswell, "Forbearance"). Gender bias was inherent in the application of this statute, and by 1848 the Texas Supreme Court regarded only threats to the life or health of the victim as cruelty. By the antebellum period (1852–61), "southern legislators and lawmakers provided greater access to divorce in order to relieve victimized and wronged wives" (Boswell, "Forbearance"). Divorce, which previously could only be granted through an act of the state legislature, was handed over to the local or judicial level. The length of time allowed before

granting an abandonment decree was shortened, cruelty cases were enlarged in scope. In 1841, Texas finally passed its divorce statute, one of the most liberal of southern divorce statutes. After its passage, "local district courts granted divorce, official abandonment occurred after three years and the cruelty clause was one of the broadest available" (Boswell, "Forbearance"). These liberalized laws resulted in higher success rates for women seeking divorce during the antebellum period.

6. As her lungs dissolve with tuberculosis, Henrietta experiences the horrific stages of the disease. As tuberculosis progresses, the blood vessels within the lungs are affected, and eventually, full hemorrhages occur, with the patient coughing up pure blood. In addition to hemorrhaging, other symptoms occur, such as an afternoon fever which falls at night, resulting in night sweats. Those affected lose weight, tire easily, and may suffer from heart palpitations as the pleura is affected. When tuberculosis is untreated, death most commonly results from inanition because the lungs are unable to bring in sufficient oxygen to nourish the body. Death may also result from drowning, as the sufferer's own body fluids flood her lungs (Caldwell 89).

7. Her last dated entry is July 14, 1861. Henrietta died June 13, 1863.

8. Her first journal, 1861–65, kept prior to her marriage, records her active reading and literary criticism of works such as *Amy Lee*, *Robinson Crusoe*, and *The Lamplighter*. Although she remarks that she likes "variety in reading" (13), Tennessee writes also of her "dislike for fictitious writings" (32).

9. Tennessee does appear in Henrietta's diary as an acquaintance and visitor to the Embree household. While references to "Tennie Keys" in Henrietta's journal are vague, Tennessee may have been employed by Henrietta to assist in household chores during her illnesses.

10. In addition to serving as her mother's comforter, Beulah is victimized in the cycle of violence in other ways. One of the most disturbing aspects of the abusive family is the transference of violent behavior. In her study on battered women, Walker found that mothers who were battered "were eight times more likely to hurt their children while they were being battered than when they were safe from violence" (*Battered Woman Syndrome* 60). Unfortunately, Tennessee is no exception, and the violence she experiences is transferred to her own daughter. On two occasions she reveals how she strikes Beulah for misbehaving and then rationalizes her own violence: "the Doctor is in a good humor which will soon dispell worse feelings from my mind, poor little B. I slaped her so hard in the face for mischief, I did not see where I was hiting suposed it not to be her front, I petted her and soon made alright with her" (May 24, 1867). In the violent environment, Tennessee struggles to repair the injury to Beulah physically as well as psychologically as she rationalizes the accidental slap, comforting her daughter as well as herself for the abuse she has inflicted. This pattern continues as Tennessee displaces her own anger toward her husband as she turns the violence on her child. Just as Beulah's companionship replaces Embree's, the child also becomes a surrogate for her mother's anger. Tennessee focuses her emotional frustration on her child: "I whiped Beulah this evening for carelessness in braking a tea cup feel sorry I did it as I think we should not be [too] hasty in inflicting punishment for accidents. I do dearly love the child and wish that God may give me wisdom to instruct her right" (December 7, 1867). Trapped in the cycle of violence, Tennessee targets Beulah at these moments of tremendous rage when "there is no one else and nothing else on which to discharge anger" (Rich 24).

11. In this, Tennessee succeeded. Beulah attended one of the most important women's academies in Texas, Baylor Female

Academy in Independence, for two years. Upon completion of her studies there, she attended the Columbia Athenaeum, in Columbia, Tennessee, graduating in 1884.

12. Unlike Henrietta, who did not seem to record any specific incident of physical violence, Tennessee writes clearly of Embree's physical abuse of Beulah. As Tennessee attempts to wean her two-year-old daughter, she records Embree's brutality as well as her helplessness: "my little Beulah kept crying for me to nurse until her Papa whipped her very hard I cryed and felt sorry for her but was too sick to do anything for her" (October 20, 1866). Her writing here may alleviate her feelings as she can explain to her daughter as well as herself why she was unable to act in Beulah's defense.

13. Intervention by neighbors was not unheard of in Texas. In a divorce hearing in Colorado County, October 15, 1848, Caroline Kahnd was granted a divorce after testifying that her husband "had taken her wearing apparel, sold it for his own use and ha[d] subsequently abused and ill-treated her by threats of violence and was only protected by the interposition of others from beatings and injury." In the divorce hearing of Marie Albrecht vs. Hubert Albrecht, September 8, 1855, the plaintiff testified that her husband had administered "a sever and cruel beating and, but for the imposition of third persons, would have greatly injured her." Albrecht's request for a divorce was denied.

14. Though divorce was available in Texas under the 1840 Act Concerning Divorce and Alimony, which allowed divorce on the grounds of cruelty "for excesses, cruel treatment, or outrages towards the other if such ill treatment is of a nature as to render their living together insupportable," women had to prove a degree of cruelty to obtain a divorce. This law also allowed husbands to bring divorce actions on more permissive grounds (Boswell "Excess and Outrages"). According to Boswell, definitions of ill

treatment involved cultural gender assumptions: "husbands need not prove much more than that their wives used profane language, had a jealous temper, or otherwise deviated from societal expectations of women, even in contested cases. By comparison, a husband could curse his wife, drive her from her home, and vent an impossible temper on her and still successfully block his wife's suit for divorce. Wives seemingly could not win contested cases unless the abuse was life-threatening" ("Forbearance").

15. Tennessee's stepdaughter, Nattie Embree, died in February 1869. She relates her stepdaughter's death after several months of silence: "June 1869. Dear old journal months weeks days have flown and no note of time or events have been committed to thy dear pages and now I dread to recall the sad things that have happened in that time of sickness and death had been in our midst poor little Nattie is with us no more on earth died February it is useless to describe how we have sorrowed after her, dear little Beulah this is to sad for me to say much on, I think you will remember her yourself for so often you speak of her, I have deferred writing for so long because I disliked to call to mind these sad things."

16. Though she had described Embree's alcoholic behavior in earlier entries, referring to his continued trips "to town," his addiction seems to have worsened over the years, and she now explains: "God alone can know the care and anxiety a wife has with a husband who has learned by habbit to indulge in drink taking" (December 20, 1883). With the acceleration of Embree's alcoholism, Tennessee faces increasing violence. Now, her dependence on her children is more than psychological. Indeed, she must turn to her fourteen-year-old son for some physical protection from his father, as she explains "oh often I feel that I turn to Russel for protection [he] is to me a great comfort" (December 20, 1883). The interference of a child was

not uncommon. In the divorce hearing of Fanny Smith vs. James Smith, August 13, 1872, Fanny Smith testified that when her husband's "passions are allowed to go unrestrained, she is subjected to such acts of violence as to cause her to be in continual jeopardy of life and limb, and when her son Ben interposes to prevent him from inflicting serious bodily harm, the defendant strikes him down and has him arrested and incarcerated in the County jail."

CHAPTER 3

1. Lizzie Hatcher Simons, typescript of diary, Barker Texas History Center, Center for American History, Univ. of Texas, Austin. The typescript contains little information concerning the journal or the author. The title page of Simons' diary notes that the text is "copied from originals in the possession of T. A. Simons, Jr. through the courtesy of Mrs. Ben E. Edwards." The typescript of Cornelia M. Noble's diary contains a letter of transmittal and comments that the original diary is owned by Dr. R. W. Noble of Temple, Texas. A letter included with the typescript indicates that Dr. Noble had also lived in San Antonio, Texas, at some point.

2. Simons never clearly indicates her county of residence; however, she seems to have been located near Port Lavaca, Texas. Port Lavaca is in Calhoun County, northeast of Corpus Christi, Texas. Lavaca Bay is protected by the Matagorda peninsula and the larger Matagorda Bay, along the Texas coast. She refers to her sugar cane harvest and most likely lived on a sugar cane plantation.

3. Hays County is located in central Texas. The county seat, San Marcos, is approximately thirty miles south of Austin and fifty miles north of San Antonio. According to the 1880 census, Cornelia Noble, Maurice Noble, and their three children —

Annie, Woods, and a female baby — were residents of Grimes County, Texas, southwest of Huntsville.

4. Cornelia M. Noble, typescript of diary, Barker Texas History Center, Center for American History, Univ. of Texas, Austin. Noble's diary is unpaginated. I have used the dates of entries for all citations.

WORKS CITED

Albrecht, Caroline, vs. Hubert Albrecht. September 8, 1855. Docket Files and Minute Records. Office of the County Clerk, Colorado County Courthouse. Columbus, Texas.

Alcoff, Linda. "Cultural Feminism Versus Post-Structuralism: The Identity Crisis in Feminist Theory." *Signs: Journal of Women in Culture and Society* 13.3 (1988): 405–36.

Allen, Martha Mitten. *Traveling West: Nineteenth Century Women on the Overland Routes.* Southwestern Studies Series 80. El Paso, Tex.: Texas Western Press, 1987.

Andreadis, Harriette. "True Womanhood Revisited: Women's Private Writing in Nineteenth-Century Texas." *Journal of the Southwest* 31.2 (1989): 179–204.

Anzaldua, Gloria. "Speaking in Tongues: A Letter to 3rd World Women Writers." In *This Bridge Called My Back: Writings by Radical Women of Color,* ed. Cherrié Moraga and Gloria Anzaldua, 165–74. New York: Kitchen Table Press, 1981.

Aptheker, Bettina. *Tapestries of Life: Women's Work, Women's Consciousness, and the Meaning of Daily Experience.* Amherst: Univ. of Massachusetts Press, 1989.

Baker, Jean Rio. "By Windjammer and Prairie Schooner, London to Salt Lake City." In *Covered Wagon Women: Diaries and Letters from the Western Trails, 1840–1890,* ed. Kenneth L. Holmes, 3: 203–81. Glendale, Calif.: Arthur H. Clark, 1984.

Baym, Nina. "At Home with History: History Books and Women's Sphere before the Civil War." *American Antiquarian Society Proceedings* 101.2 (1991): 275–95.

Bender, Barbara, ed. *Landscapes: Politics and Perspectives.* Explorations in Anthropology: University College London Series. London: Berg Publishers, 1993.

Bernikow, Louise. *Among Women.* New York: Harmony Books, 1980.

Bird, Delys. "Gender and Landscape: Australian Colonial Women Writers." *New Literatures Review* 18 (1989): 20–36.

Blodgett, Harriet. *Centuries of Female Days: Englishwomen's Private Diaries.* New Brunswick, N.J.: Rutgers Univ. Press, 1988.

Bloom, Lynn Z. "'I Write for Myself and Strangers': Private Diaries as Public Documents." In *Inscribing the Daily: Critical Essays on Women's Diaries*, ed. Suzanne M. Bunkers and Cynthia A. Huff, 23–36. Amherst: Univ. of Massachusetts Press, 1996.

Boswell, Angela. "'Excess and Outrages': Cruelty in Texas Divorce, 1840–1852." Southwestern Social Science Association. March 24, 1995.

———. "'Forbearance Ceases to be a Virtue': Divorce in Colorado County, Texas, 1837–1873." Houston Area Southern Historians Meeting. March 13, 1996.

Braxton, Joanne M. "Charlotte Forten Grimké and the Search for a Public Voice." In *The Private Self: Theory and Practice of Women's Autobiography*, ed. Shari Benstock, 254–71. Chapel Hill: Univ. of North Carolina Press, 1988.

Brée, Germaine. "Autogynography." In *Studies in Autobiography*, ed. James Olney, 171–79. New York: Oxford, 1988.

Brown, Rita Mae. *Starting from Scratch: A Different Kind of Writer's Manual.* New York: Bantam, 1988.

Bunkers, Suzanne L. "Diaries and Dysfunctional Families: The Case of Emily Hawley Gillespie and Sarah Gillespie Huftalen."

In *Inscribing the Daily: Critical Essays on Women's Diaries*, ed. Suzanne L. Bunkers and Cynthia A. Huff, 220–35. Amherst: Univ. of Massachusetts Press, 1996.

————. "'Faithful Friends': Diaries and the Dynamics of Women's Friendships." In *Communication and Women's Friendships: Parallels and Intersections in Literature and Life*, ed. Janet Doubler Ward and JoAnna Stephens Mink, 9–26. Bowling Green, Ohio: Bowling Green State Univ. Popular Press, 1993.

————. "Midwestern Diaries and Journals: What Women Were (Not) Saying in the Late 1800's." In *Studies in Autobiography*, ed. James Olney, 190–209. New York: Oxford, 1988.

————. "Subjectivity and Self-Reflexivity in the Studies of Women's Diaries as Autobiography." *a/b: Auto/Biography Studies* 5.2 (1990): 114–23.

————. "What Do Women *Really* Mean? Thoughts on Women's Diaries and Lives." In *The Intimate Critique: Autobiographical Literary Criticism*, ed. Diane P. Freedman, Olivia Frey, and Frances Murphy Zauhar. Durham, N.C.: Duke Univ. Press, 1993.

Butler, Judith. *Gender Trouble: Feminism and the Subversion of Identity.* New York: Routledge, 1990.

Caldwell, Mark. *The Last Crusade: The War on Consumption, 1862–1954.* New York: Athenaeum, 1988.

Carter, Paul. *The Road to Botany Bay: An Exploration of Landscape and History.* New York: Knopf, 1988.

Cather, Willa. *O Pioneers!* 1913. Reprint, Boston: Houghton Mifflin, 1987.

Chesnut, Mary. *The Private Mary Chesnut: The Unpublished Civil War Diaries.* Ed. C. Vann Woodward and Elisabeth Muhlenfeld. Oxford: Oxford Univ. Press, 1984.

Chodorow, Nancy J. "Gender as Personal and Cultural Construction." *Signs: Journal of Women in Culture and Society* 20.3 (1995): 516–44.

Cliff, Michelle. "Best Bet Books" *Ms.* 5.1 (1995).

Clinton, Catherine. *The Other Civil War: American Women in the Nineteenth Century.* New York: Hill and Wang, 1984.

Culley, Margo. "What a Piece of Work is 'Woman'! An Introduction." In *American Women's Autobiography: Fea(s)ts of Memory,* ed. Margo Culley, 3-31. Madison: Univ. of Wisconsin Press, 1992.

———, ed. *A Day at a Time: The Diary Literature of American Women from 1764 to the Present.* New York: Feminist Press, 1985.

Davis, Gayle R. "Women's Frontier Diaries: Writing for Good Reason." *Women's Studies* 14 (1987): 5–14.

Didion, Joan. "Why I Write." In *The Writer on Her Work*, ed. Janet Sternburg, 17–25. New York: Norton, 1980.

Dillard, Annie. *The Writing Life.* New York: HarperCollins, 1989.

Dutton, Donald C. *The Domestic Assault of Women: Psychological and Criminal Justice Perspectives.* Boston: Allyn and Bacon, 1988.

Elshtain, Jean Bethke. *Women and War.* 1987. Reprint, Chicago: Univ. of Chicago Press, 1995.

Embree, Henrietta Baker. Typescript of Diary. Barker Texas History Center. Center for American History. The Univ. of Texas, Austin.

Embree, Tennessee Keys. Typescript of Diary. Barker Texas History Center. Center for American History. The Univ. of Texas, Austin.

Ezell, Margaret J. M. *Writing Women's Literary History.* Baltimore: Johns Hopkins, 1993.

Faragher, John Mack. *Women and Men on the Overland Trails.* New Haven: Yale Univ. Press, 1979.

Faust, Drew Gilpin, "Altars of Sacrifice: Confederate Women and the Narratives of War." In *Divided Houses: Gender and the Civil War*, ed. Catherine Clinton and Nina Silber, 171–99. Oxford: Oxford Univ. Press, 1992.

————. *Mothers of Invention: Women of the Slaveholding South in the American Civil War.* Chapel Hill: Univ. of North Carolina Press, 1996.

————. "'Trying to Do a Man's Business': Slavery, Violence and Gender in the American Civil War." *Gender and History* 4.2 (1992): 197–214.

Flax, Jane. "Re-Membering the Selves: Is the Repressed Gendered?" *Michigan Quarterly Review* 26.1 (1987): 92–110.

Fothergill, Robert. *Private Chronicles: A Study of English Diaries.* Oxford: Oxford Univ. Press, 1974.

Fox-Genovese, Elizabeth. *Within the Plantation Household: Black and White Women of the Old South.* Chapel Hill: Univ. of North Carolina Press, 1988.

Franklin, Penelope, ed. *Private Pages: Diaries of American Women, 1830's–1970's.* New York: Ballantine Books, 1986.

Franz, Carol E., and Abigail J. Stewart, eds. *Women Creating Lives: Identities, Resilience, and Resistance.* Boulder, Colo.: Westview Press, 1994.

Frawley, Maria H. *A Wider Range: Travel Writing by Women in Victorian England.* London: Associated Univ. Presses, 1994.

Freedman, Diane P. "Border Crossing as Method and Motif in Contemporary American Writing, or How Freud Helped Me Case the Joint." In *The Intimate Critique: Autobiographical Literary Criticism*, ed. Diane P. Freedman, Olivia Frey, and Frances Murphy Zauhar, 13–22. Durham, N.C.: Duke Univ. Press, 1993.

Fuller, Margaret. *Summer on the Lakes.* In *The Portable Margaret Fuller*, ed. Mary Kelley, 69–227. New York: Viking Penguin, 1994.

Gilman, Charlotte Perkins. *The Living of Charlotte Perkins Gilman: An Autobiography.* 1935. Reprint, ed. Ann J. Lane, Madison: Univ. of Wisconsin Press, 1990.

Gilmore, Leigh. *Autobiographics: A Feminist Theory of Women's Self-Representation.* Ithaca, N.Y.: Cornell Univ. Press, 1994.

Glasgow, Ellen. *Barren Ground*. 1925. Reprint, New York: Harcourt Brace, 1985.

———. *The Woman Within: An Autobiography*. 1954. Reprint, ed. Pamela R. Matthews. Charlottesville: Univ. Press of Virginia, 1994.

Godwin, Gail. "A Diarist on Diaries." *Antaeus* 61 (1988): 9–15.

Hadley, Amelia. "Journal of Travails to Oregon." In *Covered Wagon Women: Diaries and Letters from the Western Trails, 1840–1890,* ed. Kenneth L. Holmes. Vol. 3: 53–96. Glendale, Calif.: Arthur H. Clark, 1984.

Hampsten, Elizabeth. *Read This Only to Yourself: The Private Writings of Midwestern Women, 1880–1910*. Bloomington: Indiana Univ. Press, 1982.

———. "Tell Me All You Know: Reading Diaries and Letters of Rural Women." In *Teaching Women's Literature from a Regional Perspective*, ed. Leonore Hoffman and Deborah Rosenfelt, 55–63. New York: Modern Language Association, 1982.

Hassam, Andrew. "'As I Write': Narrative Occasions and the Quest for Self-Presence in the Travel Diary." *Ariel* 21.4 (1990): 33–47.

Hoffman, Leonore, and Margo Culley, eds. *Women's Personal Narratives: Essays in Criticism and Pedagogy*. New York: Modern Language Association, 1985.

Hogan, Rebecca. "Engendered Autobiographies: The Diary as a Feminine Form." In *Autobiography and Questions of Gender*, ed. Shirley Neuman, 95–107. London: Frank Cass, 1991.

hooks, bell. "Writing from the Darkness." *Triquarterly* 75 (1989): 71–77.

Hyde, Anne Farrar. *An American Vision: Far Western Landscape and National Culture, 1820–1920*. New York: New York Univ. Press, 1990.

Hymer, Sharon. "The Diary as Therapy: The Diary as Adjunct to Therapy" *Psychotherapy in Private Practice* 9.4 (1991): 13–30.

Jaffe, Peter G., David A. Wolfe, and Susan Kaye Wilson. *Children of Battered Women*. Developmental Clinical Psychology and Psychiatry 21. London: Sage Publishers, 1990.

James, Henry. *The Portrait of a Lady*. 1881. Reprint, New York: Bantam Books, 1983.

Jeffrey, Julie Roy. "'There is Some Splendid Scenery': Women's Responses to the Great Plains Landscape." *Great Plains Quarterly* 8 (1988): 69–78.

Jelinek, Estelle. *The Tradition of Women's Autobiography: From Antiquity to the Present*. Boston: Twayne, 1986.

————, ed. *Women's Autobiography: Essays in Criticism*. Bloomington: Indiana Univ. Press, 1980.

Jones, Dorothy. "Mapping and Mythmaking: Women Writers and the Australian Legend." *Ariel* 17 (1986): 63–86.

Judith. *The New English Bible*. The Apocrypha. Oxford: Oxford Univ. Press, 1970.

Juhasz, Suzanne. *Reading from the Heart: Women, Literature and the Search for True Love*. New York: Viking, 1994.

————. "'Some Deep Old Desk or Capacious Hold All': Form and Women's Autobiography." *College English* 39.6 (1978): 663–68.

Kahnd, Caroline, vs. Jacob Kahnd. October 15, 1848. Docket Files and Minute Records. Office of the County Clerk, Colorado County Courthouse. Columbus, Texas.

Kellogg, Ronald. *The Psychology of Writing*. Oxford: Oxford Univ. Press, 1994.

Kolodny, Annette. *The Land Before Her: Fantasy and Experience of the American Frontiers, 1630–1860*. Chapel Hill: Univ. of North Carolina Press, 1984.

LeJeune, Philippe. "'The Journal de Jeune Fille' in Nineteenth Century France." Trans. Martine Breillac. In *Inscribing the Daily: Critical Essays on Women's Diaries*, ed. Suzanne M. Bunkers and

Cynthia A. Huff, 107–22. Amherst: Univ. of Massachusetts Press, 1996.

Lensink, Judy Nolte. "Expanding the Boundaries of Criticism: The Diary as Female Autobiography." *Women's Studies* 14 (1987): 39–53.

Miller, Dale T., and Carol A. Porter. "Self-Blame in Victims of Violence." *Journal of Social Issues* 39.2 (1983): 139–52.

Mills, Sara. *Discourses of Difference: An Analysis of Women's Travel Writing and Colonialism.* London: Routledge, 1991.

Milton, John. *Paradise Lost.* In *John Milton: Complete Poems and Major Prose*, ed. Herritt Y. Hughes, 173–469. New York: Macmillan, 1957.

Morgan, Sarah. *Sarah Morgan: The Civil War Diary of a Southern Woman.* Ed. Charles East. New York: Simon and Schuster, 1991.

Morrison, Toni. *Beloved.* New York: Knopf, 1987.

Moynihan, Ruth Barnes. *Rebel for Rights: Abigail Jane Scott Duniway.* London: Yale Univ. Press, 1983.

Myres, Sandra L. *Westering Women and the Frontier Experience, 1800–1915.* Albuquerque: Univ. of New Mexico Press, 1982.

Noble, Cornelia M. Typescript of Diary. 2R128. Barker Texas History Center. Center for American History. Univ. of Texas, Austin.

Personal Narratives Group. *Interpreting Women's Lives: Feminist Theory and Personal Narratives.* Bloomington: Indiana Univ. Press, 1989.

Phelps, Elizabeth Stuart. *The Story of Avis.* New Brunswick, N.J.: Rutgers Univ. Press, 1985.

Pratt, Mary Louise. "Scratches on the Face of the Country; or, What Mr. Barrow Saw in the Land of the Bushmen." *Critical Inquiry* 12.1 (1985): 119–43.

Rable, George. "Missing in Action: Women of the Confederacy." In *Divided Houses: Gender and the Civil War*, ed. Catherine Clinton and Nina Silber, 134–45. Oxford: Oxford Univ. Press, 1992.

Rich, Adrienne. *Of Woman Born: Motherhood as Experience and Institution.* 1986. Reprint, New York: Norton, 1995.

Robinson, Roxana. *Georgia O'Keefe: A Life.* New York: Harper, 1990.

Schlissel, Lillian. *Women's Diaries of the Westward Journey.* New York: Schocken Books, 1982.

Scott, Abigail Jane. "Journal of a Trip to Oregon." In *Covered Wagon Women: Diaries and Letters from the Western Trails, 1840–1890*, ed. Kenneth L. Holmes and David C. Duniway, 5:21–138. Glendale, Calif.: Arthur H. Clark, 1986.

Scott, Anne Firor. *Natural Allies: Women's Associations in American History.* Chicago: Univ. of Illinois Press, 1991.

Scott, Joan Wallach. "Experience." In *Feminists Theorize the Political*, ed. Judith Butler and Joan W. Scott, 22–40. New York: Routledge, 1992.

Silko, Leslie Marmon. *Ceremony.* New York: Viking Press, 1977.

Simons, Judy. "Invented Lives: Textuality and Power in Early Women's Diaries." In *Inscribing the Daily: Critical Essays on Women's Diaries*, ed. Suzanne M. Bunkers and Cynthia A. Huff, 252–63. Amherst: Univ. of Massachusetts Press, 1996.

Simons, Lizzie Hatcher. Typescript of Diary. 2R178. Barker Texas History Center. Center for American History. Univ. of Texas, Austin.

Sizer, Lyde Cullen. "Acting Her Part: Narratives of Union Women Spies." In *Divided Houses: Gender and the Civil War*, ed. Catherine Clinton and Nina Silber, 114–33. Oxford: Oxford Univ. Press, 1992.

Smith, Fanny, vs. James Smith. August 13, 1872. Docket Files and Minute Records. Office of the County Clerk, Colorado County Courthouse. Columbus, Texas.

Smith, Sidonie. *A Poetics of Women's Autobiography: Marginality and the Fictions of Self-Representation.* Bloomington: Indiana Univ. Press, 1987.

Smith-Rosenberg, Carroll. *Disorderly Conduct: Visions of Gender in Victorian America.* New York: Oxford Univ. Press, 1985.

Stanley, Liz. *The Auto/Biographical I: The Theory and Practice of Feminist Auto/Biography.* Manchester, England: Univ. of Manchester Press, 1992.

Stanton, Domna C. "Autogynography: Is the Subject Different?" In *The Female Autograph: Theory and Practice of Autobiography from the Tenth to the Twentieth Century,* ed. Domna C. Stanton, 3–20. Chicago: Univ. of Chicago Press, 1984.

Stewart, Abigail J. "Toward a Feminist Strategy for Studying Women's Lives." In *Women Creating Lives: Identities, Resilience, and Resistance,* ed. Carol E. Franz and Abigail J. Stewart, 11–35. Boulder, Colo.: Westview Press, 1994.

Temple, Judy Nolte, and Suzanne L. Bunkers. "Mothers, Daughters, Diaries: Literacy, Relationship, and Cultural Context." In *Nineteenth Century Women Learn to Write,* ed. Catherine Hobbs. Feminist Issues: Practice, Politics and Theory, ed. Alison Booth and Ann Lane. Charlottesville: Univ. Press of Virginia, 1995.

Tompkins, Jane. "Me and My Shadow." In *The Intimate Critique: Autobiographical Literary Criticism,* ed. Diane P. Freedman, Olivia Frey, and Frances Murphy Zauhar, 23–40. Durham, N.C.: Duke Univ. Press, 1993.

———. *Sensational Designs: The Cultural Work of American Fiction, 1790–1860.* Oxford: Oxford Univ. Press, 1985.

Torgovnik, Marianna. "Experimental Critical Writing." *ADE Bulletin* 96 (1990): 8–10.

Walker, Lenore E. *The Battered Woman.* New York: Harper and Row, 1979.

———. *Battered Woman Syndrome.* New York: Springer Publishing Company, 1984.

Walker, Nancy. "'Wider than the Sky'": Public Presence and Private Self in Dickinson, James and Woolf." In *The Private Self:*

Theory and Practice of Women's Autobiography, ed. Shari Benstock, 272–303. Chapel Hill: Univ. of North Carolina Press, 1988.

Weir, Allison. *Sacrificial Logics: Feminist Theory and the Critique of Identity.* New York: Routledge, 1996.

Whites, LeeAnn. "The Civil War as a Crisis in Gender." In *Divided Houses: Gender and the Civil War*, ed. Catherine Clinton and Nina Silber, 3–21. Oxford: Oxford Univ. Press, 1992.

———. *The Civil War as a Crisis in Gender: Augusta, Georgia, 1860–1890.* Athens: Univ. of Georgia Press, 1995.

Woolf, Virginia. "The Legacy." In *A Haunted House and Other Stories,* 126–35. New York: Harcourt Brace Jovanovich, 1944.

———. "Moments of Being." In *A Haunted House and Other Stories,* 103–11. New York: Harcourt Brace Jovanovich, 1944.

———. *A Room of One's Own.* New York: Harcourt Brace Jovanovich, 1929.

———. "A Sketch of the Past." In *Moments of Being,* 61–159. 1976. Reprint, ed. Jeane Schulkind, New York: Harcourt Brace, 1985.

Yinger, Robert J., and Christopher M. Clark. "Reflective Journal Writing: Theory and Practice." Occasional Paper, no. 50. The Institute for Research on Teaching. East Lansing, Mich.: Michigan State Univ., 1981.

Zauhar, Frances Murphy. "Creative Voices: Women Reading and Women's Writing." In *The Intimate Critique: Autobiographical Literary Criticism*, ed. Diane P. Freedman, Olivia Frey, and Frances Murphy Zauhar, 103–16. Durham, N.C.: Duke Univ. Press, 1993.

INDEX

abuse, physical, 57, 70, 74–75; of
    Beulah Embree, 76–77, 141n;
    and community action, 142n;
    and divorce, 142n; effect on
    children, 138n; emotional, 75;
    examples of, 142n; physical and
    psychological, 51–52, 54, 56,
    59, 71, 75, 77; protection from,
    142–43n; psychological, 126;
    revelations of, 70, 76–77; and
    transference, 141n
academic discourse, xviii
Act Concerning Divorce and
    Alimony, 141–42n
act of writing, xiv–vi, xxiii–iv, xxxvi,
    123–24, 129, 132
acts of meaning, 132
adapting to place, 8, 47
aesthetic terms, 18
agency, xxiv, xxv, xxviii, 57, 80–81,
    124, 130, 132; methods of, xv
Alcoff, Linda, xxix–xxx
alcoholism, details of, 143n
Allen, Martha Mitten, 8
American landscape as Divine, 45
Andreadis, Harriette, 58
anti-slavery attitudes, 37–38, 136n
Anzaldua, Gloria, 48
Aptheker, Bettina, xxvii–iii, 52

audience, 62
authenticity of experience, xxviii
auto/biography, 54
autobiographical agency, 53
autobiographical production, 53
autobiographical writing, 51, 90
autobiographics, 53
autobiography, xxviii, 124; as resist-
    ance, 52–53
autonomy, 124–25

Baker, Jean Rio, 11, 30–46, 126;
    view of American Democracy,
    41–43; arrival in U.S., 36; diary
    audience, 40; family group, 30;
    sense of identity, 31, 40; leaving
    home, 32; on the Overland trail,
    40; reaction to death, 34–35;
    response to Utah, 31; sea voy-
    age, 31–36; sense of displace-
    ment, 46; sense of place, 33;
    sense of self, 41, 43.
battered woman syndrome, 51,
    138n
battered women, 58, 65, 78, 138n;
    and characterological blame, 62,
    71–72; and self blame, 69–70;
    "perceived control," 58
Battle of Corinth, 101

She Left Nothing in Particular was designed and typeset on a Macintosh computer system using Quark software. The text and chapter openings are set in Brontë. This book was designed and typeset by Bill Adams and manufactured by Thomson-Shore, Inc. The paper used in this book is designed for an effective life of at least three hundred years.